DEDICATED TO:

GOOD BOOKS

TO HELP MAKE

THE GOOD LIFE

BETTER.

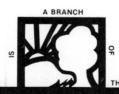

A BRANCH

IS          OF

THE GOOD LIFE PRESS          THE CHARING CROSS PUBLISHING COMPANY

FAMILY TREE

# HOW TO OUTSMART YOUR LANDLORD
## (If You're A Tenant)

# OR

# HOW TO OUTSMART YOUR TENANT
## (If You're A Landlord)

AN UNDERSTANDABLE OUTLINE
OF LANDLORD-TENANT LAW

by

STUART J. FABER

a landlord,
a tenant,
and a lawyer

GOOD LIFE PRESS

*A Division of the Charing Cross Publishing Company*
658 South Bonnie Brae Street
Los Angeles, California 90057
(213) 483-5832

# Author's Note

The purpose of this book is to take the mystery out of the law. You need not be afraid of the law. On the contrary, you should realize that it can help and protect you, if you ask it to. This book will give you the knowledge and understanding you need to make the law serve you.

This book will not make a lawyer out of you. If you use this book as a substitute for sound legal advice or to debate with your lawyer, then I have failed. If you use it to enlighten yourself about your legal rights and as a tool in cooperating with your lawyer should you need one, then I will consider the book a success.

Laws differ from state to state and, indeed from situation to situation. In addition, they change from time to time. Therefore, use this book not as a bible, but as a guide.

Remember—law is designed for *you*. Acquaint yourself with it, employ it intelligently and you will prevail.

*Stuart J. Faber*

# TABLE OF CONTENTS

# About the Author

Stuart J. Faber is an active California lawyer. He received his bachelor's degree from the University of Wisconsin and his Doctor of Laws degree from Loyola University. Since 1960 he has maintained an active law practice in Los Angeles.

In writing for the public, Mr. Faber has provided a much needed service. "The legal profession," he says, "seems intent on keeping a smokescreen between the public and knowledge of the law." Recognizing the need to take the mystery out of the law, Mr. Faber has written a number of books based on his legal expertise and experience. His publications have included "How to Defend Traffic Tickets," "Landlord-Tenant Law— A Coexistence Manual," books on drug laws, divorce law and law for the elderly.

# INTRODUCTION

To be sure, landlords and tenants have certainly done their share to increase court congestion. Indeed, without them, the courts would be pretty empty places. For some reason an undue amount of animosity and misunderstanding frequently exists among landlords and tenants.

Why is it that the landlord is so often visualized by the tenant as a wealthy, unfeeling landowner whose only interest is to get the rent and give little in return? Why is it that the tenant, in the eyes of the landlord, frequently is seen as a second class citizen who, at any time, might destroy the landlord's property and run off without paying the rent?

Similar attitudes are not as prevalent between people in other business relationships. Rarely does such animosity exist, for example, between consumer and grocer, insured and insurer, or patient and doctor.

So why is it so difficult for landlords and tenants to get along?

The answer to this is somewhat of a mystery. Perhaps it is that the transaction between landlord and tenant is a more permanent and lasting one. The tenant, forking over to the landlord month after month what is perhaps his largest installment expenditure, is exposed to him for a longer period of time than is the consumer who enters a store, purchases an article, and leaves the store. Landlords are frequently more knowledgeable about the intricacies of landlord and tenant law (or at least think they are) because they deal with these laws every day. Some landlords will, on occasion, attempt to intimidate a tenant with this supposed knowledge of the law. The tenant reasons that the landlord must be knowledgable or he wouldn't own a piece of real estate. So, the tenant is intimidated. But the landlord's attempts to intimidate may backfire. The tenant may become stubborn, refuse to pay the rent, and refuse to move.

This book is designed to acquaint both landlords and tenants with a working knowledge of landlord-tenant law. Hopefully, this knowledge will enable you to know where you stand, to be secure in stating your position, and to stand up for your rights. Hopefully, this knowledge will also enable you to be able to decide when *not* to stand up for your rights but just to try and get along.

The thesis of this book is how to outsmart each other. Frequently the best way to outsmart each other is to stop fighting. But if you must fight, let this book be part of your arsenal.

1

The author, who is a lawyer and who has been both a landlord and a tenant, has seen all sides of the picture and has experienced feelings in each capacity. One important thing the author has gained from this experience is that some knowledge of the other person's legal position, as well as one's own, can do wonders in alleviating fears, distrust and misunderstanding. The reduction of these emotions can help in establishing a better relationship between landlord and tenant.

The other important thing the author has learned is that knowledge of the other person's legal position, as well as one's own, can do wonders in equipping one with a shelter against a legal disaster in the future.

A word of caution. The laws in many of our states in the area of landlord and tenant relationships are fairly uniform. You should, however, check the laws of your state to determine if there are any which are inconsistent with those described in this book.

If you have any doubts about your legal position, if you are presently faced with a serious problem, by all means, consult your attorney. He is the best person to advise and guide you in a difficult situation.

# CHAPTER ONE
## Some General Concepts

This, the first chapter in the book, was actually the last one to be written.

It contains some general concepts of landlord-tenant law which do not appropriately fit in other parts of the book or which perhaps do not contain sufficient volume to justify a chapter to themselves. The chapter might also contain some material which the author forgot to include elsewhere.

What follows, however, is not to be underestimated, for the tidbits herein present some of the problems common to most landlord-tenant situations.

Tommy Tenant, one of the heroes of this book, looks at an apartment. He likes it. He wants to rent it. He asks Larry Landlord, the other hero (the author will not take sides) to hold the apartment for him for two days until he gets his pay check. He gives Larry Landlord $10 to hold it for him. Has Tommy rented the apartment or does he merely have the right to rent it in the next two days? It depends upon the intent of the parties. The best way to make sure that the true intent of the parties is properly expressed is to spell it out in a receipt. Both Tommy and Larry should demand a receipt because it offers protection to both of them.

If the receipt states that the $10 is only a deposit to hold the apartment for two days, then the prospective tenant has, in effect, "taken an option." The receipt has created the following legal rights between the parties:

A.  If Tommy doesn't rent the apartment in two days, he loses his $10.

B.  If he doesn't rent the apartment in two days, the prospective landlord cannot sue him for the rent.

C.  If he does rent the apartment within two days, the $10 will not apply to the rent unless it was previously agreed that it would apply.

D.  The prospective landlord cannot rent the apartment to anyone else for the two-day period.

Suppose the $10 receipt states that the $10 is a part payment on the first month's rent. Suppose the first month's rent is $100. Such a receipt creates the following legal rights between the parties:

A.　A landlord-tenant relationship has already been created. The month starts from the date of the delivery of the $10. If the tenant does not come up with the $90 in two days, not only does he lose his $10 but he can be sued for the $90.

B.　The tenant must give notice to vacate (even though he has not taken possession) in a manner as discussed in Chapter 9.

C.　The landlord cannot rent the apartment to someone else for the two-day period.

D.　The $10 will apply to the rent.

E.　The tenant in this situation is entitled to possession immediately unless the receipt states otherwise.

Some landlords like to take a deposit and still reserve the right to rent to someone else who might come along between the time the tenant pays the deposit and the time he actually accepts the apartment. This is not an unreasonable position to want to be in. The prospective tenant may never come back. True, the landlord has his $10, but he might have lost another tenant in the meantime. If he gives a receipt for the $10 and states that the receipt constitutes an offer of the tenant to rent the apartment, and *not* partial rent or a deposit, then, until the landlord accepts the offer he is not obligated to rent to that person. The landlord may, in the interim, rent to someone else, but if he does he must return the $10.

He must also return the $10 if the prospective tenant demands it at any time prior to the landlord's acceptance of his offer. If he does accept the offer before the tenant withdraws it, however, the landlord has then rented him the apartment.

Now, let's suppose that in any of the above situations the tenant comes back in two days and the parties reach some agreement and the prospective tenant is now officially the tenant of the apartment.

It will be drummed into the reader again and again throughout this book that it is of utmost importance, whether the tenancy is on a month to month basis or is a yearly lease, that the parties put in writing what they expect of each other during the rental period. This should be done even before the deposit is given.

Later we will discuss in considerable detail exactly what a lease or rental agreement should contain, so let's assume at this point that the written agreement has been made and that possession is about to pass to the tenant.

The landlord must make the premises available to the tenant. It is not the obligation of the tenant to see to it that the premises are available for possession. Previous tenants must have been already removed by the landlord and the premises must, in all respects, be available for occupancy. The tenant has no obligation to begin his rent payments in the absence of such availability.

Possession means exactly what the term denotes. The tenant is entitled to exclusive possession of the property. The landlord, in the absence of an agreement to the contrary, has no right of entry for any purpose. He does not have the right to rent or show the premises to another.

The tenant's right to possession extends only to those portions of the premises actually described in the agreement. This is one argument in favor of a written agreement. The agreement should clearly describe just what areas are being rented.

The right to possession carries with it the right to use the premises for any lawful purpose. Any restrictions must be spelled out in the written agreement. The leased premises become the castle of the tenant as long as the tenant abides by the terms of the lease or rental agreement.

The landlord is required to insure the tenant's right to the quiet use and enjoyment of the premises. This means that the landlord cannot unduly bother or harass the tenant or cause other tenants to disrupt his quiet enjoyment. A violation of tenant's right to the quiet use and enjoyment can result in the tenant's suing the landlord for damages. He could also sue the landlord for cancellation of the lease.

A tenant, of course, should not be allowed to invade the quiet enjoyment of other tenants or of the landlord (if the landlord lives on the premises). The lease or rental agreement should provide that such an invasion by the tenant would constitute grounds for eviction.

The tenant is required to pay the rent on the date due. The landlord is entitled to demand cash and is not required to take a check.

The landlord is not required to accept less than the entire amount of rent due. He may refuse a partial payment and proceed to evict a tenant for nonpayment of rent.

A landlord is required to give the tenant a receipt when the rent is paid. The tenant should always demand one, especially when the rent is paid in cash. The landlord should always keep a duplicate receipt.

Unless it is expressly or impliedly agreed, rent is payable at the *end* of each month. This may come as quite a surprise. Custom and usage are usually sufficient to create the implication that rent is payable at the beginning of the month (especially since a tenant always pays before he moves in) so there is really little to worry about as far as a landlord is concerned.

If a tenant moves out in the middle of a month and has paid in advance for a full month, he is not entitled to a refund. He would be entitled to a refund, however, if his rent were payable at the end of the month.

What happens if the tenant, in a lease situation, wants to sublease in the middle of the lease period?

In the absence of a provision in the lease to the contrary, the tenant may assign or sublet without the consent of the lessor.

What is the difference between an assignment and a sublease?

In an assignment situation, the tenant passes all of his interest to another party. He reserves no remaining portion of the lease to himself and the relationship of landlord-tenant no longer exists between the original tenant and the landlord. In a sublease, the original tenant retains some interest. Either he retains the right to re-enter at some time during the remaining term or he continues to occupy some portion of the premises.

If a lessor does not want the tenant to have the right to assign or sublet, he must declare this in the lease or rental agreement. The wording must be specific. If the lease merely states that the tenant cannot assign or sublet, and the tenant attempts to do so anyway, the assignment or sublease is not void. In this situation, if the landlord accepts rent from the new tenant, the assignment or sublease becomes valid and binding.

Code of Civil Procedure Section 1161.4 provides that if the tenant assigns or sublets in the presence of a provision in the lease forbidding such action, the landlord is entitled to terminate the lease. See Chapter 9. But the right to terminate may be waived if the landlord accepts rent from the new tenant.

Be sure in a lease, if you are a landlord, to prohibit assignments *and* subleases. A prohibition against assignments alone is not sufficient to prohibit subleases.

The best way to prevent a sublease or assignment is to state that any attempt to sublease or assign will be *void*. The use of the magic word "void" prevents the assignee (the person to whom assigned) or the sublessee (the person to whom subleased) from having any rights against the landlord.

A sublease or assignment does not relieve the original tenant from paying rent to the landlord unless the landlord agrees in writing to relieve the original tenant and accept rent only from the new tenant. A landlord, however, would be foolish to do this. A landlord might be willing to go along with a sublease if the new tenant is financially responsible and both the original tenant and the subtenant agree in writing to be responsible for the rent.

Frequently a lease contains a provision that a landlord will not unreasonably withhold consent to an assignment or sublease. Such a provision creates many problems. What is reasonable? It is often necessary to go to court to find out. By the time this takes place the lease has probably already expired. Therefore, such a provision can benefit only a landlord because he can always withhold consent for some alleged "reasonable" excuse. Tenants, therefore, if they contemplate the possibility of a sublease during the period of their lease, should demand an unlimited right to sublease or assign.

As you will see later it might be desirable to provide in a lease that a tenant has a right to sublet. Failure to afford him this right can deprive you of certain benefits if he abandons the property. (See Chapter 9.)

Leases may be extended or renewed. An extension is the spreading out or stretching of the original lease. A renewal contemplates the making of a new lease.

A lease may be extended merely by writing on the old lease, "This lease is extended until _____, 1973," or to whatever date it is to be extended. The notation should be initialed by both parties.

Renewals usually arise out of options. The tenant, if he desires to exercise his option to renew, must express this desire in writing before the expiration of the lease. Then, either a new lease must be drawn or the landlord and tenant must, in writing, agree that the old lease shall be extended on the original terms (if that is their desire).

If a lease is not extended or renewed and the tenant does not vacate at the end of the term, what happens? The landlord can sue to evict the tenant. But if he allows the tenant to remain in possession, the relationship between the landlord and tenant becomes that of a month to month tenancy. See paragraph XXV in Chapter 2.

Throughout this book references will be made to sections of the Landlord-Tenant Law of California. California laws are divided into codes, such as the Civil Code, Code of Civil Procedure, Penal Code, Education Code, etc. A group of codes is that body of law which deals with a certain class of subjects. The Penal Code, for instance, deals with crimes, criminal procedure and crime prevention. Some laws overlap into several codes. This book will deal primarily with the Civil Code and with the Code of Civil Procedure. The codes are broken down into sections; for example, Civil Code Section 1942 deals with the duties of the landlord with respect to repairs of the leased premises. Each section is called a law or a statute. Civil Code Section 1942, therefore, is a statute or law found in a book called the Civil Code.

The codes which affect landlord-tenant have been set out in the Appendix of this book. The Civil Codes will each be proceeded by the abbreviation, "CC" and the Codes of Civil Procedure by "CCP."

It is suggested that you read the code sections. Legislators have a way of taking a simple subject and transforming it into complex language in the form of the written law. But by sifting out the "whereases" and "wherefores" the code sections should become quite clear to you.

It's a great technique in dealing with an obstinate landlord or tenant to point out the law to him. It not only will show him that his position is not a sound one legally but it also has the psychological effect of showing him who is the better informed of the two.

Laws vary from state to state. The author has used the California Codes as a general model. Most states have similar laws. However, you should check your state laws to make sure they are not different.

Frequently, the author refers to the term "action" or "cause of action." A cause of action is a legal term which means that one party has the right to sue another for a wrong that the other has committed. Thus, if the tenant has not paid his rent, the landlord has a cause of action, or the right to sue the tenant for rent. Similarly, if the landlord has wrongfully evicted the tenant, the tenant may have a cause of action against the landlord for wrongful eviction, or forcible entry.

The term "judgment," as used in this book, refers to the award a court may give one party against another. Thus, if A sues B for $100 and

A wins, A then has a judgment against B for $100.

The chapters which follow cover subjects which most frequently present problems to landlords and tenants.

Unfortunately, every problem could not be anticipated and it is hoped that the very problem with which you might be concerned has not been omitted.

# CHAPTER TWO
## Creation Of The Tenancy

Whenever you have rented or leased an apartment, house, store, office, warehouse, vacant land, mobile home, or any structure which is attached to the land, you have created a tenancy. The landlord can also be referred to as the lessor and the tenant can also be referred to as the lessee.

There are many types of tenancies. We will, however, be dealing only with two types in this book: namely, a month to month tenancy and a tenancy for a fixed term. The month to month tenancy means exactly what it says. That is, the lessee rents the premises for one month at a time. The lease for a fixed term exists when the premises are rented for a specific period of time. The period could be anywhere from one day to 100 years or more.

Tenancies for a period of one year or less are enforceable even if they are created by oral agreement. The problem with oral agreements, of course, is that the spoken word is more difficult to prove than the written word. That problem brings us to what the author considers the most important message of this book: *ALWAYS PUT IT IN WRITING!* Do this every time you create a tenancy. Do this if the tenancy is for only one day! Do this if the tenancy is for 10 years! Do this if the tenancy is for one month! Do this if you are a landlord! Do this if you are a tenant!

Here is a typical scene: The setting, small claims court; the characters, Larry Landlord, Tommy Tenant, and Judge Solomon.

Larry Landlord: "Your Honor, Tommy Tenant keeps parking his car in garage no. 4 and when he rented the apartment, I told him that he must use garage no. 2."

Tommy Tenant: "Your Honor, Larry Landlord told me that I could have garage no. 4 when the other tenant moved out, but in the meantime I should use garage no. 2."

Larry Landlord: "Your Honor, that's a lie, I never said that."

Judge Solomon: "Well, I wasn't there when Tommy Tenant rented the apartment; how am I supposed to know who is telling the truth?"

### THE END

How much easier it would have been if Larry Landlord and Tommy Tenant had a rental agreement in which it was simply stated: "Tommy

Tenant shall have the use of garage no. 2, but as soon as the present tenant using garage no. 4 moves out, Tommy Tenant may have the use of garage no. 4."

If you learn nothing else from this book, remember to put all rental agreements in writing. Leases for more than one year must, of course, be in writing. Many people don't realize, however, that month to month tenancies should also be in writing. Putting them in writing is not a difficult task. Lease forms and month to month rental agreements are readily obtainable in stationery stores. An example of a month to month tenancy form can be found in the Appendix. Additions to the forms can easily be handwritten on the back of the form.

The language of the additions need not be "lawyeristic." Any verbiage which conveys the intent of the parties is sufficient.

Always insist that the other party enter into a written agreement. If a person isn't willing to put his promises in writing, that's a good indication that he has no intention of carrying his promises out.

So if you really want to outsmart your landlord or your tenant, negotiate a good written agreement. Then, if later there is a dispute as to what was previously agreed on, you can point to the written document and say, "Ah ha! Look what you signed here."

We will now embark on an enumeration of a quantity of additional paragraphs which should be added to the printed form which you have purchased.

Depending on whether you are a tenant or a landlord, you should try and have included in your agreement any of the following paragraphs which will obviously strengthen your position. You should attempt to have excluded from the agreement any of those paragraphs which will obviously weaken your position.

The additions, whether written on the back or on a separate attached sheet, are called an "addendum." The addendum, if not written on the back, may be stapled to the printed form. Somewhere on the printed form there should be written: "This agreement is subject to the attached addendum." Or, "This agreement is subject to the addendum written on the back." Each party should sign both the printed form and the addendum and each party should receive a copy of each of the documents.

Following is a list of clauses which should be added to the printed form. With less obvious ones, I will indicate which party would benefit from the clause.

I. "In the event of a default by lessee, the tenancy shall be forfeited and any holding over thereafter shall be construed as a month to month tenancy for the same rental as stated above."

This provision benefits a landlord. Without it a court could permit a tenant to remain under the lease if the tenant paid the amount owing within five days. This provision could also benefit a tenant because if he wanted to break his lease he could stop paying the rent. Then, if the landlord declared a forfeiture of the lease, the tenant would not be responsible for further payments on the lease beyond the period during which he remained in possession. This provision is applicable only to leases.

II. "If either party is required to file suit to enforce any of the provisions of this agreement, the prevailing party shall be entitled to reasonable attorney's fees."

This provision is of benefit to either party, depending upon who is suing whom. Attorney's fees cannot be awarded by a court without such a written provision.

III. *"Landlords' liens.* In addition to those rights of lessor as set forth in Sections 1861 and 1861a of the California Civil Code, Lessee agrees that any expenses incurred by Lessor under the terms hereof in connection with any termination of this Lease or breach of or default under the terms, covenants and/or conditions hereof by Lessee, including reasonable attorney's fees of Lessor, and including any expenses incurred by Lessor pertaining to the repair or alteration of the premises, reasonable wear and tear excepted, shall be deemed to be 'proper charges due' from Lessee under the provisions of said Sections and shall be part of the basis for any such lien. In addition to any other rights and/or remedies available to Lessor hereunder, Lessor may apply any amounts recovered from the enforcement of said lien, under the provisions of said Sections, to the payment of any amounts due to Lessor hereunder.

In addition to the above, Lessor shall have a lien upon the automobile or automobiles of Lessee, if any, at any time garaged and/or parked on the premises, for any 'proper charges due' from Lessee as described in Sections 1861 and 1861a of the California Civil Code, or as described herein and Lessor shall be entitled to enforce said lien against said automobile or automobiles as provided in said Sections of the California Civil Code."

Probably not enforceable, but it could have great psychological effect.

IV. "If lessor's right of reentry is exercised following the abandonment of the premises by lessee, then lessor may consider any personal property belonging to lessee and left on the premises to also have been abandoned, in which case lessor may dispose of all such property in any manner he shall deem proper."

This provision allows a landlord to enter the property without a court action after the property has been abandoned by the tenant and to sell the property at public sale after storing it for 30 days. C.C.P. 1174. This applies only when the property has been abandoned. However, see Chapter 9 for new changes.

V. "Lessee hereby agrees that as of the date of this lease the premises are in a good and tenantable condition, that he will take good care of the premises and appurtenances, including any household furniture or other personal property belonging to lessor and covered by this lease, and that lessee, as part of the consideration for rental stated above, will at his sole cost and expense keep and maintain said premises, appurtenances and personal property in good and sanitary condition and repair during the term of this lease. All damage or injury done to the premises by lessee or any person who may be on the premises with lessee's consent shall be paid for by lessee, and lessee shall at the termination of this lease surrender to lessor the said premises with the appurtenances and all household furniture and other personal property belonging to lessor in as good condition and repair as when received, reasonable and proper use thereof and damage by fire or the elements excepted."

This paragraph shifts the burden of repair to the tenant and could relieve the landlord of his duties under Sections 1941 and 1942. There are, as yet, no court decisions which have ruled that this provision would or wouldn't be valid. See Chapter 5.

VI. "Either party may terminate this tenancy by giving not less than seven days written notice of his intention to do so."

This provision applies only to month to month tenancies and could be useful either to a landlord who might in the future be anxious to get rid of a tenant or to a tenant who might be anxious to terminate his tenancy. It could backfire, however, if the tenant did not want to get out in seven days or if the landlord did not want the tenancy to end in such a short period. It is difficult when you make the agreement to know how you will feel in the future. In the absence of this provision, a landlord or a tenant must, in a month to month tenancy, give at least 30 days' written notice to terminate the tenancy. (See C.C. 1946)

VII.   Prepaid rent. The following example is based upon a one year lease at $100 per month.

"The rent for the term of this lease shall be the sum of $1200 payable as follows: $300 payable on January 1, 1971, and the sum of $100 per month beginning on February 1, 1971, and on the first day of each month thereafter until the whole of said sum has been paid."

This clause benefits a landlord since prepaid rent is not refundable unless the tenancy is wrongfully terminated by the landlord.

VIII.   "The rental shall be $100 per month, plus an additional $100 as consideration for this lease."

This clause may benefit a landlord since the additional $100 would not be refundable. Tenants beware of such a clause. See Chapter 3.

IX.   "In the event of any breach of this lease by lessee, then lessor, besides other rights or remedies he may have, shall have the immediate right of reentry and may remove all persons and property from the premises. If lessee breaches this lease and abandons the premises before the end of the term, or if lessee's right to possession is terminated by lessor because of a breach of the lease, then in either such case lessor may recover from lessee all damages suffered by lessor as the result of lessee's failure to perform his obligations hereunder, including, but not restricted to, the worth at the time of the award (computed in accordance with Paragraph (B) of Section 1951.2 of the California Civil Code) of the amount by which the rent then unpaid hereunder for the balance of the lease term exceeds the amount of such rental loss for the same period which the lessee proves, could be reasonably avoided by lessor."

Under the new law on leases executed after July 1, 1971, the landlord, if tenant abandons, can re-let the premises and cannot keep the property vacant for the remainder of the lease. See Civil Code Section 1951.2.

X.   "Landlord may, at his option, allow the lease to remain in full force and effect and sue the tenant for the monthly rental payments as they become due."

This addition is the result of the new Civil Code Section 1951.4. Landlord can leave the property vacant and sue for the rent, but only if he has, in the lease, given tenant the right to sublet or assign the lease. Since the landlord may not want to give tenant the right to sublet or assign, there may be more disadvantages to including this paragraph than advantages. A landlord is better off, if a tenant abandons the premises, to try and re-rent the premises and sue tenant for the difference. Vacant properties do not produce income.

XI.   "In the event the tenant breaches the terms of this agreement or abandons the property, lessor shall have the right to enter and remove all persons and property therefrom. Lessor shall further have the right to enter the premises from time to time for purposes of inspecting and/or showing to prospective tenants or purchasers."

This certainly benefits a landlord and tenants should try to have it excluded. Landlords, however, even with the presence of this provision, are limited by the Forcible Entry and Detainer Laws. Be sure to read Chapter 7.

XII.   "The attached drawing shall become a part of this agreement and the area so designated therein shall be the area to which tenant is entitled to possession."

This may be useful in a situation where the area leased is difficult to describe without a drawing or map. You may attach a drawing and have it initialed by each party.

XIII.   "Tenant shall be entitled to the use and exclusive possession of garage number 4 and locker number 4 in the basement."

XIV.   "In the event that lessor cannot deliver possession by the commencement of the lease period, the lease shall remain in full force and effect and the commencement date shall be extended to the date of possession and the period of the lease shall run from that date."

This protects landlords. The absence of this provision would allow tenant to cancel the lease if possession of the property were not delivered on time.

XV. "Tenant shall not commit waste upon the premises and shall be liable for treble damages in the event of such waste."

See Code of Civil Procedure Section 732.

XVI. "Tenant shall not use the leased premises in violation of any state, federal, county or local law nor break any such law within the leased premises. Tenant shall use the premises only as a dwelling. The dwelling is rented to no more than two persons."

A good "lease breaker" for landlord if tenant, for example, uses narcotics or serves alcohol to minors in his apartment. It is also a good lease breaker if the tenant works part time out of his apartment or if he takes in another roommate.

XVII. "Tenant shall have the option to renew this lease for a period of one more year on the same terms and conditions. To exercise this option, tenant shall give written notice of his desire to continue as a tenant at any time before the expiration of this lease."

This assures the tenant of at least a two year lease without originally obligating himself to two years. He signs up for a year and at his option, at any time before the end of the first year, can extend the lease an additional year.

XVIII. "Landlord agrees to make all necessary repairs on the premises when so notified by tenant and shall be permitted on the premises to make such repairs."

An important addition for the tenant. If the landlord fails to make the repairs, he is then liable to the tenant for injuries that the tenant might suffer as a result of a defect which was not repaired. See Chapter 5.

XIX. "The furniture and other equipment included in this lease includes the following: _____"

XX. "Either party can terminate this lease at any time by giving 30 days' written notice if any of the following events occur: (list events)."

An option to terminate based upon the occurrence of certain events not within the control of the person exercising the option is permissible.

One could not use his own act as a basis for exercising the option. To allow that would require only that one commit the act and then profit by his own wrong. A provision, for example, allowing a *tenant* to terminate a lease if *landlord* rented an adjoining apartment to a tuba player would be permissible. But to allow *landlord* to exercise the option by renting to a tuba player would be ludicrous. All the landlord would have to do if he wanted to terminate tenant's lease would be to rent the adjoining apartment to a tuba player.

Would you believe that a California court ruled that a provision in a lease was valid which gave a landlord an unlimited right to terminate a lease? The lease also stated that the landlord did not have to give any reason for his intention to terminate but could do so at his whim.

Notice the effect of this decision. If a landlord can terminate at any time, the tenant, in effect, has no lease at all. He is really a month to month tenant.

The case said nothing about whether such a provision would be valid if it reserved the right to terminate to the tenant.

The name of the case is *Wagner vs. Shapano*. The author disagrees with the court in that case. But since that case appears to be the law, the following paragraph is suggested if you want a complete escape clause:

XX(a). "The landlord may, with or without reason, terminate this lease at any time by the giving of seven (7) days written notice to the tenant."

Tenants, if you can get away with it, try to have a similar provision inserted giving you the same right. Who knows, a court may uphold it.

XXI. "Unless lessee shall give to lessor written notice, not less than sixty days prior to the expiration date of the above-mentioned term, of lessee's election to terminate this lease on said date, this lease shall automatically renew and continue for an additional term at the expiration of the original term, or any renewal thereof, upon the same terms and conditions as set forth herein until terminated by such notice in some ensuing term. Lessor shall be entitled to terminate this lease upon like notice to lessee at like times."

Be sure to read Chapter 4 on more detailed requirements necessary to make this paragraph enforceable. Also, see Civil Code Section 1945.5.

XXII. "Cleaning fee is non-refundable and does not include special cleaning such as shampooing the carpeting, cleaning furniture, or sending out drapes to be cleaned. It does include cleaning the apartment, cleaning mattress, stove, refrigerator, fan, windows, sweeping the carpet, polishing the furniture, and supplying new furnace filters. If the cleaning charges exceed the amount of the cleaning fee, the difference may be deducted from the security deposit or charged directly to the lessee."

XXIII. "Security Deposit: Lessee agrees to deposit with lessor the amount of _____ Dollars ($ ___) to secure lessee's faithful compliance with each and every term and condition of this lease and to secure lessee's faithful performance of all acts and things required of lessee by the covenants and agreements made herein. Said deposit is not, nor shall it be deemed to be, the installment amount due under the terms hereof for any calendar month. At the termination of this lease, for any reason whatsoever, said deposit, or so much thereof as is reasonably necessary, shall be applied to any premises whether resulting from any damage to the premises or lessee's use thereof, in order to ready said premises for re-rental. In addition thereto, lessor may retain, use or apply said deposit, or so much thereof as is reasonably necessary, to any debt owed to lessor by lessee, or to cure any breach or default by lessee hereunder, or to compensate lessor reasonably for any expenses incurred or damages suffered by reason of any such breach or default hereof by lessee.

Upon termination of this lease for any reason whatsoever, should the balance of the security deposit in the possession of lessor be insufficient for any of the purposes stated in this paragraph, lessor shall be entitled to proceed with collection of any such deficiency in such manner and through such means as lessor deems advisable.

If this lease is terminated for any reason whatsoever prior to the expiration of twelve (12) months after commencement of the first term hereof, except by the mutual consent of lessor and lessee, any portion of said security deposit remaining after the deduction of that amount necessary to ready said premises for re-rental as aforesaid, shall be deemed to be liquidated damages for the compensation of lessor for potential expenses connected with re-renting said premises. This applies even if term of lease is less than twelve (12) months.

Lessee shall not be entitled to any interest on the security deposit and lessor shall have the right to commingle said security deposit with other funds of lessor.

Should lessor sell the entire premises, lessor may deposit with the purchaser thereof the unexpended or unappropriated funds deposited by lessee, and thereupon lessor shall be discharged from any obligation, responsibility or liability for such funds.

Should any deduction be made from the security deposit, as provided for in this lease, lessor may proceed as follows: Lessor shall be entitled to serve a notice upon lessee declaring the amount by which said security deposit has been reduced. Said notice shall require that lessee pay to lessor that amount of money necessary to make the present balance equal to the original balance thereof. Should lessee fail or refuse to comply with the terms of said notice within three (3) days after service thereof, lessee shall be in breach of and in default under the terms and conditions of this lease and lessor shall be entitled to proceed against lessee in the manner set forth herein.

Should lessee comply with all of the terms and conditions of this lease, the balance of the security deposit remaining, after the accomplishment of those things set forth herein, shall be returned to lessee. In no event shall any such refund be made prior to the expiration of thirty (30) days after the termination of this lease. Acceptance by lessee of any such refund, whether by the cashing of lessor's refund check, or otherwise, shall be deemed to be a full and final release of lessor by lessee of any and all actions, causes of action, claims, demands, damages, costs, expenses of any nature whatsoever arising out of or in any way connected with lessee's occupancy of the premises. The apartments are painted on a five (5) year basis, and the drapes, carpeting, and furniture cleaned on a three (3) year basis. Lessor shall not be obligated to clean or paint anything in apartment should lessee's occupancy exceed three (3) to five (5) years, respectively. Mattresses are cleaned each time tenancy of apartment changes. Lessee is required to furnish his own mattress covers and in the event the mattress cannot be cleaned to a like-new condition (no spots or stains), lessee agrees to pay the price of a new mattress. Lessee agrees and shall be required to keep a neat, clean apartment, which includes but is not limited to cleaning the windows when they become dirty and keeping the filter changed in the furnace. Failure to do the latter will result in a carbon stain on walls and/or ceiling and may result in the whole apartment having to be painted at lessee's expense. Lessee agrees lessor's condition report dates and data will be controlling factors in any dispute and together with statements by in-coming lessee will be final and binding on outgoing lessee for security deposit refund purposes."

If you desire a security deposit provision instead of prepaid rent, this is an acceptable provision.

XXIV. *"Assignment:* Lessee shall not assign this lease, or any part thereof, or any right or privilege appurtenant thereto, or suffer any other person (the agents and servants of lessee excepted) to occupy or use said premises, or any portion thereof, without the written consent of lessor first had and obtained, and a consent to one assignment, subletting, occupation or use by any other person, shall not be deemed to be a consent to any subsequent assignment, subletting, occupation or use by another person. Any such assignment or subletting without such consent shall be void, and shall, at the option of lessor, terminate this lease. This lease shall not, nor shall any interest therein, be assignable, as to the interest of lessee, by operation of law, without the written consent of lessor."

See Chapter 1.

XXV. *"Holdover.* Should lessee remain in occupancy of the leased premises after the date of termination of this lease by notice or mutual agreement, at lessor's election, such holdover shall be deemed to create a month to month tenancy. All other terms and conditions of this lease shall remain in full force and effect between lessor and lessee."

This was discussed in Chapter 1 and Chapter 4.

XXVI. *"Occupancy Receipt.* Lessee acknowledges that lessee has examined the leased premises, and the appurtenances thereto, and knows the condition thereof and the nature of the services and utilities, if any, provided therewith, and agrees that the same are in good and sanitary order, condition and repair, except as specifically set forth in the occupancy receipt to be executed by lessee upon acceptance of occupancy of the leased premises. Lessee agrees to execute such occupancy receipt upon acceptance of occupancy of said premises, which occupancy receipt shall be attached hereto and incorporated herein by reference. Lessee agrees to set forth in said occupancy receipt each and every exception to the good order, condition and repair of the leased premises, whether patent or latent, and agrees further that from and after the execution thereof lessee will not assert against lessor any exception of the good order, repair and condition of the leased premises not set forth in said occupancy receipt. Should lessee not execute said occupancy receipt or, after execution thereof, fail to take possession of the leased premises, it shall be conclusively presumed, in any legal action or other dispute between lessor and lessee that said premises were at all material times in good order, condition and repair, without exception or reservation of any nature whatsoever."

See Chapters 5 and 6. A tenant should not agree to this provision.

XXVII. *"Facilities:* If lessor shall furnish to lessee any storage space, laundry space or facility, or any other space or facility in or about the premises, the same shall be deemed to be furnished by lessor under a revocable license.

If washing machines and/or other equipment are made available to lessee, the same shall be used upon condition that lessor shall not be liable for such equipment, nor for any injury to lessee and/or damage to lessee's personal property, resulting from the use thereof by lessee or any other person, and that lessee's use and/or operation of any such washing machines and/or other equipment, or presence while such are being used and/or operated by any other person, is at lessee's sole cost, risk and/or expense, whether such washing machines and/or other equipment are furnished gratuitously or for hire, or otherwise.

In the event of any injury or damage, as hereinabove described, lessee agrees to hold lessor harmless and indemnify lessor."

This paragraph would allow a landlord to take away a tenant's garage privileges at any time.

XXVIII. *"Pets.* Lessee shall not permit any cat, dog, parrot or other animal to be housed in or about the leased premises without the written consent of lessor. Lessor shall be entitled to revoke such consent at any time by giving notice to lessee of such revocation. Should lessee fail or refuse to remove any such animal(s) from the premises within three (3) days after the giving of such notice, lessor, in addition to any other rights and/or remedies available to lessor hereunder, without notice to lessee, may deduct the amount of Ten Dollars ($10.00), per day, or any portion thereof from the security deposit made by lessee, for each day that said breach and/or default continues."

XXIX. *"Services.* Lessor shall not be liable for, nor shall there be any abatement of rent, nor any claim of eviction, constructive or otherwise, by reason of:

1.   Any interruption, failure or curtailment of the heat, water supply, electric current, elevator service or any other service to be supplied by lessor to lessee;

2.   Any injuries or damages caused by the elements, or the acts or inactions of any other person in or about the entire premises;

3.   Any injuries or damages caused by gas, electricity, water, rain or snow in or on the entire premises and the buildings located thereon, or from any of the pipes, drains, conduits, radiators, boilers, tanks, appliances or equipment therein;

4.   Any interference with light, air, view or other interests of lessee, or the taking of any space to comply with any law, ordinance, governmental regulation or court order."

XXX.   *"Destruction.* In the event of (A) a partial destruction of said premises or the building containing same during said term which requires repairs to either said premises or said building, or (B) said premises or said building being declared unsafe or unfit for occupancy by any authorized public authority for any reason other than lessee's act, use or occupation, which declaration requires repairs to either said premises or said building, lessor shall forthwith make such repairs, provided such repairs can be made within sixty (60) days under the laws and regulations of authorized public authorities, but such partial destruction (including any destruction necessary in order to make repairs required by any such declaration) shall in no way annul or void this lease, except that lessee shall be entitled to a proportionate deduction of rent while such repairs are being made, such proportionate deduction to be based upon the extent to which the making of such repairs shall interfere with the lessee's occupation of said premises. If such repairs cannot be made within sixty (60) days, lessor may, at his option, make same within a reasonable time, during which this lease will remain in full force and effect. In the event that lessor does not so elect to make such repairs which cannot be made within sixty (60) days, or such repairs cannot be made under such laws and regulations, this lease may be terminated at the option of either party. In respect to any partial destruction (including any destruction necessary in order to make repairs required by any such declaration) which lessor is obligated to repair or may elect to repair under the terms of this paragraph, the provisions of Section 1932, Subdivision (2), and Section 1933, Subdivision (4), of the Civil Code of the State of California are waived by lessee. A total destruction (including any destruction required by any authorized public authority) of either said premises or said building shall terminate this lease."

See Chapter 9.

Lessor has a right to enter the premises at reasonable hours for inspection.

Lessor may terminate this lease upon 30 days written notice in the event he sells the property.

If a tenant wants to make certain that his lease will not be terminated by a sale of the property (in the absence of the above provision), he should record the lease with the country recorder. This puts any buyer on notice of his lease. To record the lease the signature of the lessor must be notarized.

Not all of these provisions will, of course, be necessary in every situation. Some obviously apply only to leases and not to month to month tenancies.

There are two other topics which should be discussed in connection with the preparation of a lease or rental agreement.

If a landlord is insecure about the tenant's ability to pay the rent, the landlord should insist on someone, perhaps a parent or other responsible person, to guarantee the agreement. It does not have to be someone who will reside on the premises. It gives the tenant an extra incentive to pay the rent. If the tenant doesn't pay, the landlord can always go against the guarantor. The following is suggested:

"I guarantee the full performance (including but not limited to the payment of rent) of all of the terms and conditions of this agreement."

Be sure to have the guarantor sign the agreement.

It is also important to have the agreement signed by the spouses, both the landlord's and the tenant's.

There are two reasons for this. The first is that a spouse's separate property standing in his or her own name would not be vulnerable to a court judgment unless the spouse signed the agreement.

The second reason, which would apply only to leases in excess of one year, is that a husband could, in California, break a lease if his wife had not signed. This is because an agreement involving real estate for a term in excess of one year must be executed by the husband and wife in order to be binding in California.

The balance of the book will contain other suggestions as to lease additions. It is sometimes difficult to anticipate what events will arise in the future, but try and think of everything and don't be afraid to insist on its being placed in the agreement.

Remember that certain provisions may be put into a lease to make it look frightening, but they will nevertheless be totally unenforceable.

They include:

1. Waiver of security deposit restrictions;

2. Waiver of right to keep landlord out of dwelling at certain times;

3. Waiver of right to have landlord keep premises in habitable condition or to exercise reasonable care to avoid injury to tenants or their property.

Even if a right may be waived, the waiver is void unless the lease is presented to the tenant before he moves in. These rules apply to most dwelling leases which were signed after January 1, 1976.

# CHAPTER THREE
## Prepaid Rent Vs. Security Deposits

The landlord must make the decision at the time he rents or leases to a tenant whether, in situations where he demands more than one month's rent, he should accept the excess of the initial payment as prepaid rent or as a security deposit. There are advantages and disadvantages to either decision.

First of all, by "excess" I refer to the amount the landlord receives over the stated monthly rental. So if the monthly rental is $100 and, at the beginning of the lease, the landlord gets a $200 initial payment, $100 is the excess.

Prepaid rent (which is usually the last month's rent) becomes the immediate property of the landlord upon its receipt and is not refundable to the tenant unless the landlord wrongfully terminates the tenancy. The landlord may keep prepaid rent where a tenant wrongfully abandons a property even though the prepaid rent exceeds the amount due the landlord.

A disadvantage in accepting prepaid rent vs. a security deposit is that the prepaid rent is taxable income to the landlord at the time of its receipt. Another disadvantage is that prepaid rent can be kept by the landlord only for one purpose; that is, for nonpayment of rent. It cannot be forfeited and retained for other violations of the lease or rental agreement. If a landlord desires to have the excess declared as prepaid rent, he should clearly state that intent in the lease or rental agreement. Under the new law, effective January 1, 1978, there are strict rules on security deposits.

Section 1950.5, which applies only to dwelling units, defines security as any payment or fee, including an advance payment of rent, that is used for:

1. Compensation for default in rent;

2. Repair of damages to premises caused by tenant;

3. Cleaning of premises upon termination of the tenancy.

No matter what the parties label the deposit, an amount no greater than two month's rent may be demanded in the case of unfurnished property. An amount up to three month's rent may be demanded for furnished property. An advance payment of six months' rent may be demanded if the lease is for six months or more. The landlord and tenant may also agree to the payment of an advance amount to be used for furnishing, decorating or repairs by the landlord.

How much of the security may the landlord retain? Only an amount necessary to compensate the landlord for defaulted rent, to repair damages, or to clean the premises. No amount may be retained for ordinary wear and tear. What is ordinary wear and tear? If the parties can't agree, a court will have to decide.

What happens when the tenancy is terminated? The landlord, within two weeks, must furnish the tenant with an itemized written statement of the basis for retaining any part of the security and return the balance. If the landlord sells the property, or otherwise is divested of ownership, he must transfer the security to the new owner and thereafter notify the tenant. Or, he may return the security to the tenant.

A bad faith retention of the security may subject the landlord to a penalty of $200, plus other damages if the tenant can establish them.

No lease or rental agreement may contain a provision characterizing a deposit as nonrefundable.

The rules are similar to tenancies involving nonresidential property. The only significant difference is that there are no restrictions on the amount of advance security that can be demanded.

One advantage of a security deposit is that it remains the property of the tenant and is not taxable income to the landlord until the landlord asserts a claim to it for some violation of the tenancy. Another advantage of the security deposit is that the security deposit can be retained for violations of the lease or rental agreement other than the failure to pay rent.

There is another advantage to having a security deposit rather than prepaid rent. The right to bring an unlawful detainer action will not arise until all the rent has been exhausted, but since the security deposit is not considered rent, the unlawful detainer action can be commenced at any time after rent becomes due even though the landlord holds a security deposit. But if the excess was designated as prepaid rent, until that rent is applied to the amount owed, the landlord could not begin an unlawful detainer action.

How should the respective clauses be worded? Suppose the rent is $100 monthly.

Here is an example of a prepaid rent clause:

"Receipt of $200 is hereby acknowledged, $100 of which is to apply to the first month's rent, the balance of which is to be applied as a security deposit and is subject to the security deposit provisions of this agreement." (See Chapter 2, paragraph XXIII, for the more detailed addition on security deposits.)

Here is an example of a first and last month's rent clause:

"Receipt of $200 is hereby acknowledged. $100 of which is to apply to the first month's rent, the balance of which is to apply to the last month's rent."

One way a landlord might get around the restriction on the amount of security deposit is to charge a greater amount for the first months' rent. Another method is to charge a bonus for renting or leasing the premises. Here are a few examples:

1. Amount of rent. The monthly rental shall be as follows: $300 for the first months' rent and $150.00 for the second through the twelfth month. Tenant hereby pays the sum of $600.00, which constitutes payment for the first, second and last month.

2. Bonus. Tenant hereby pays landlord the sum of $600.00. Three hundred dollars is consideration for the execution of this lease; $150 is for first months' rent, $150 is for last months' rent.

Remember that cleaning deposits come under the protection of the new security deposit laws. A landlord can retain only those amounts necessary for the cleaning of the apartment. A recent case held that a landlord had to refund a "non-refundable" cleaning deposit. Notwithstanding the fact that the tenant signed an agreement waiving his right to a refund, he was entitled to the refund unless the landlord could establish that the tenant knew of his rights under the refund law.

# CHAPTER FOUR
## Termination And Changes In The Tenancy

Tommy Tenant wants to move. He occupies an apartment on a month to month basis. When he moved in on March 1, he paid a month's rent in advance and paid on the first day of each month thereafter. He paid his rent on November 1 and it is now November 30. Thinking he is all paid up, he moves without notice.

Larry Landlord tries to rent the apartment and does so on December 15. He then sues Tommy Tenant for rent from December 1 to December 15. Does Tommy Tenant have to pay?

This question presents one of the most misunderstood areas of landlord-tenant law. Before the end of the chapter the question will be answered.

In this chapter we will deal with the questions of the termination of tenancies, only as they relate to instances where the tenant is not in default or where the landlord has not been guilty of some wrongdoing. The questions we will deal with are: "What must the tenant do if he wants to move, and what must the landlord do if he wants the tenant to move?"

The simplest answer is found in a lease. A lease for a year, for instance, expires one year after it began. So the tenant, at the conclusion of the year, merely moves unless a new agreement has previously been entered into between himself and the landlord. Neither the landlord nor the tenant is required to give notice. The landlord is entitled to assume that the tenant will move.

What happens if the tenant does not move? In the absence of a new written agreement, the tenant is considered to be "holding over" as a month to month tenant (assuming the landlord accepts the rents and allows him to do so) at the same monthly rental as he was paying under the lease. If the rent is payable yearly, it is presumed that the holding over is for another year, but in most cases where the rent is payable monthly, the holding over is from month to month only. See Civil Code Section 1945. Also, see Chapter 2, paragraph XXV.

In one situation, a lease is automatically renewed. In 1966, Civil Code Section 1945.5 was added which provides that a lease is automatically renewed if the tenant either: (1) fails, before the expiration to give notice of his intention not to renew, or (2) remains in possession after expiration.

This automatic renewal takes place only if the lease so provides for it. The lease must contain the provision in the body of the document and again immediately prior to the place where the tenant signs the lease. The wording, which is found in Chapter 2, must be in at least eight-point bold face type. See paragraph XXI in Chapter 2.

So, tenants, be sure you read your lease, because many tenants are surprised at the end of the year when they become aware of this provision for the first time and they find themselves stuck for another year. *It's no excuse that you didn't read your lease!*

Now let's turn to month to month tenancies.

A month to month tenancy is automatically renewed at the end of each month for another period of 30 days. To terminate a month to month tenancy, a tenant or landlord (whoever wants to terminate the tenancy) must give 30 days *written* notice of his intention to terminate. The tenant is responsible for rent only for 30 days after the notice unless he stays in possession beyond 30 days after the notice was given.

If a tenant fails to give notice, he is liable for rent for up to 30 days after he abandons the premises. If, during that 30 day period the landlord rents the property, the tenant is liable only for the period between the time he abandoned and the time the property was re-rented. So, in our example, Tommy Tenant would be liable up to December 15. If Larry Landlord had not re-rented the apartment, Tommy would be liable for 30 days' additional rent.

Suppose Tommy Tenant had given notice on November 15. Since his responsibility extends for 30 days from the time he gives notice, he would be responsible for the rent until December 15, even though he moved on November 30 (unless Larry re-rented the apartment on December 1).

How about a landlord? He must also give 30 days' notice if he wants a tenant to move. Until the notice is properly given, the tenant may remain in possession. He must vacate no later than 30 days after the notice is properly given to him.

The law also allows either party to give notice to terminate at any time, not just at the beginning of the month. Suppose a tenant rented an apartment on September 8. The first month ends on October 7. A new month begins on October 8 and ends on November 7. The tenant could, for example, give notice on September 29 and be responsible for rent *only* until October 28. It would be advisable in this situation that he give the notice on September 29 and then, on October 8, pay the landlord a prorated amount of rent from October 8 to October 28.

A landlord and tenant can provide in a lease, or in a month to month agreement, that some notice less than 30 days is all that is required for a termination. Section 1946 of the Civil Code, which deals with the subject of notice, provides that the parties may agree in writing to a period of not less than seven days for the giving of a notice to terminate.

The rules already discussed in this chapter generally apply to changes in the lease or rental agreement as well as to termination. In a lease, of course, the one party cannot, during the term of the lease, make any changes unless the lease allows for such changes or unless both landlord and tenant mutually agree to the change in writing.

But in a month to month tenancy, if a landlord decides to raise the rent or make any other changes, he must do so by giving 30 days written notice of said change.

May a tenant, when he gives 30 days' notice to terminate, allow his last month's rent (if he, at the beginning of the tenancy paid first and last months' rent in advance) to apply? Yes, if the rental agreement provided that the amount which the tenant paid at the beginning was to be construed as first and last months' rent. But if the payment was intended as a security deposit, the tenant must pay the last month's rent when it falls due and obtain a refund of the security deposit after he moves. So, for tenants it is always better in a month to month situation to have the first rental payment construed as first and last months' rent. Refer back to Chapter 3 for the proper form of designating prepayments to be last month's rent.

Many tenants are shocked when they do not pay rent for the last month because they think that their security deposit will apply. The landlord could forfeit the security deposit for the failure of the tenant to pay rent and still demand a last month's rent. A tenant can protect himself by providing in the agreement that if, when he gives notice to terminate, he is not in default in the payment of rent, his security deposit can be applied to the last month's rent.

How should the notice to terminate to the landlord be worded? There is no required form, but here is a suggestion:

"To Larry Landlord:

You are hereby notified that I will vacate the premises within 30 days from the date of this notice.

Dated: January 15, 1972

*Tommy  Tenant"*

If a landlord wishes to have a tenant move, the following is suggested:

"To Tommy Tenant:

You are hereby notified that you must vacate the premises by September 1, 1972.

Dated: July 31, 1972.

*Larry  Landlord"*

For an example of a notice regarding an intention to increase the rent, see the Appendix.

This question always arises, "Can landlord show the premises to prospective tenants after tenant has given notice to terminate? No, unless the rental agreement or lease so provides, the landlord has no right in either a lease or a month to month tenancy to enter the premises of the tenant.

What is the proper method of serving the notices? The notices shall be personally delivered or sent by certified or registered mail to the landlord or the agent of the landlord to whom the tenant had previously paid his rent.

For other methods of service of the notice, consult Section 1162 of the Code of Civil Procedure. This section is located in the Appendix.

Tommy Tenant, happily putting the dishes in the dishwasher one night, jauntily flicks the switch and is met with silence. The dishwasher doesn't work. He calls Larry Landlord to fix it. Larry says, "You fix it."

Who fixes it?

The general rule is that the landlord is not required to make any repairs to the leased premises. The tenant is said to "take the property as he finds it." Not only must the tenant make the repairs (if he wants the thing repaired) but he must do so at his own expense.

There are two exceptions to the general rule:

A. If the landlord, in the lease or rental agreement, agreed to make the repairs, and

B. If the thing needing repair falls under Section 1941 of the Civil Code.

The first exception presents another argument in favor of putting things in writing. If Tommy Tenant had insisted upon a provision in his lease that all repairs must be made by landlord, the landlord would have been obligated to fix the dishwasher.

The second exception is more complicated. Section 1941 of the Civil Code is fully set out in the Appendix. Briefly, it requires a landlord, in a building intended for occupation by human beings, to keep the premises in a tenantable condition.

What constitutes the making of a building untenantable is set forth in Section 1941.1 of the Civil Code? (See Appendix). Basically, that section requires the presence of sufficient waterproofing, adequate plumbing facilities, and water, heating and electrical equipment, all in good working order. A broken dishwasher would probably not qualify under this section, so Tommy Tenant would have to fix it.

The landlord's duty is limited if the tenant does not live up to certain obligations. Section 1941.2 of the Civil Code requires the tenant to keep the premises in a clean and sanitary condition and to properly use and maintain the premises and all its electrical, gas and plumbing fixtures. The tenant's neglect or abuse of the premises could deprive him of his rights under Civil Code 1941.

What happens if repairs (such as would qualify under Civil Code

1941) were needed and the landlord refused to make them? The tenant, after giving reasonable notice to the landlord, may himself make the repairs, or have them made, and may, in any 12 month period, deduct up to one month's rent for the expenses of such repairs. The tenant may also, if he elects, move from the premises and, upon doing so, is discharged from further payment of rent.

Prior to 1970, a tenant could waive his rights under the foregoing sections, but now such a waiver would be void. But an indirect way to secure a waiver might be accomplished by inserting a provision in the rental agreement in which tenant agrees to make all repairs as part payment of his rent. (See Chapter 2, paragraph V.)

Does the landlord have the right to enter the premises in order to make the repairs? Yes, but only if the repairs are those required under Civil Code Section 1941. If the landlord desires to enter the premises for the purpose of making more extensive repairs or alterations, he may not be allowed to do so unless the lease or rental agreement authorizes his entry.

The difficult question is whether, in a specific case, the thing requiring repair falls under the list of the items in Section 1941.1 of the Civil Code. It is urged that you read and study Section 1941.1 very carefully if the question ever arises.

A recent *Hinson vs. Delis*, decided in 1972, held that violations of city housing codes, if the violations affect habitability, can result in suspending the tenant's duty to pay the rent. The court adopted its "implied warranty" theory, in effect stating that the landlord agreed to keep the premises in a livable condition. This case seems to give ammunition to the tenant even beyond that given in Section 1941.

What happens in the event of a partial or total destruction of the property? If the property is totally destroyed, the lease is of course automatically terminated. If there is a partial destruction and the tenant remains on the property and continues to pay the rent, he has admitted that the property is tenantable and cannot thereafter recover for damages sustained because the landlord failed to repair.

Now let's talk about alterations. Can the tenant make alterations on the leased property? He can if the alterations are minor and do not change or damage the leased premises to any extent. Again, the safe thing to do would be to have a provision in the lease which sets forth the extent to which the tenant will be allowed to make repairs or alterations.

Who receives the improvements after the termination of the lease? Unless there is an agreement in the lease to the contrary, the improvements, if they have become an integral part of the premises and are fixed to the premises, become the property of the landlord. If the improvements can be removed without injury to the building, the tenant can remove them unless they have become an integral part of the premises. For example, suppose the tenant cuts a hole in a wall and installs a window. The window has become an integral part of the building. Even if tenant is willing to remove the window and replace the wall in its original condition, he cannot do so. Suppose the tenant installs a bookcase to a wall. Since this is not an integral part of the building, he may remove the bookcase even though the removal may result in injuries to the building. He will, however, be responsible for the repair of those injuries. Since it is not always easy to determine what is or is not an integral part of the building, it is best to set forth in the lease a list of the anticipated improvements to be made by the tenant. It is also advisable in the lease to agree to what will be the ultimate disposition of the improvements.

A very important topic most favorable to tenants relative to repairs is that of retaliatory eviction. This topic is so new and so important that it will be discussed in a separate chapter. (See Chapter 11.)

# CHAPTER SIX
## Injuries To Tenants And Their Guests

One day, Tommy Tenant was shown an apartment by Larry Landlord. While being shown the apartment Tommy noticed a loose board on a stairway leading to the balcony. He called this to Larry's attention. "Yep," said Larry, "I've got to fix that one of these days."

Later, after Tommy Tenant rented the apartment, he was walking up the stairs. The board, loose as it was, broke under the weight of his foot. His leg went through the hole, causing him severe injuries. Is Larry Landlord liable for Tommy Tenant's injuries?

The law is replete with general rules. The rules are stated with great care, then mutilated with exceptions. The law regarding the liability of landlords for injuries to tenants is no exception (in that it has many exceptions).

The general rule is that the landlord is not liable for injuries sustained by a tenant on the rented premises. Californians: See end of Chapter. California does not follow the general rule.

Now, here come the exceptions. The landlord is liable if:

A.   He had knowledge of the dangerous or defective condition; or

B.   The condition existed for so long that he should have had knowlege of it; or

C.   He agreed in the lease or rental agreement to make repairs and failed to do so; or

D.   He reserves a portion of the leased premises to himself and allows a defective condition to exist; or

E.   He makes repairs but does so in such a negligent manner that the repaired object causes an injury to the tenant.

It would seem from the exceptions that at least as to patent defects, that is, defects which are readily discoverable, the landlord has some duty to discover the defects and to repair them.

The landlord is under no duty, however, to examine the property for latent defects.

A latent defect is one which is not readily apparent through casual observation. Since the landlord has no duty to discover the latent defects, his lack of knowledge of them through failure to discover will ordinarily relieve him of responsibility for injuries which are sustained as a result of such defects.

If, however, the landlord knows of latent defects and permits the tenant to occupy the premises without informing him of the presence of such defects, the landlord in this case would be liable.

It would be advisable for a tenant to have it stated in the lease or rental agreement that the landlord has inspected the property and represents that no latent defects exist. In such a case it is believed that the tenant could rely upon such representations and hold the landlord responsible for any injuries that might be sustained as a result of the defects.

Does the tenant have any duty to inspect the property for latent defects? If defects could be discovered by the tenant through reasonable inspection, the tenant would have a duty to discover them. If they are not reasonably discoverable, then, of course he has no duty. His failure to discover the defects would not deprive him of his right to damages from the landlord. But if the tenant, when he takes possession of the premises, is aware of such defects, he then assumes the risk of the dangerous condition and cannot recover for damages. Thus, Tommy Tenant would be out of luck in our example.

But suppose the landlord had contracted to repair the defects and failed to do so. In this case the landlord would be liable even if tenant knew of the defective condition.

A different rule applies to defective conditions where the defect exists in a part of the premises that is under the landlord's control or which is reserved for the use of all of the tenants. In this case the landlord has a duty to make reasonably careful inspections at proper intervals and to see that the common areas are kept in a safe condition. This applies to latent and patent defects. Examples of common areas would be stairways, hall ways, lobbies and elevators. It would appear that an agreement in which the tenant waives his right to damages for injuries sustained in common areas (of the building, not his body) would be void.

A landlord would not be liable for injuries sustained by a tenant where the defective condition was caused by the tenant or where the tenant used the property in a manner not contemplated by the lease.

What about a landlord's duty to third persons, that is, guests or invitees of the tenant? Generally, as to those parts of the premises exclusively occupied by the tenant, the landlord has no responsibility to the third party. He is not even required to warn him of obvious defects or dangers. The tenant himself is under the duty to exercise care to said persons.

There are two possible exceptions:

A.  The landlord will be liable if the injury occurs in those areas over which the landlord has some control, such as hall ways.

B.  The landlord will be liable if he contracted to keep the premises in good repair. The landlord must know of the defective condition, however, and be given a reasonable opportunity to correct it.

Suppose a tenant is injured as a result of a defect in personal property, such as a chair. The rule is somewhat different.

Furniture supplied to a renter of a furnished apartment must be in a safe condition at the time of the rental; otherwise, the landlord is liable for injuries sustained.

The California court recently, in the case of *Fakhoury vs. Magner*, said that a landlord would be held strictly liable for injuries caused by such defects. In the *Fakhoury* case the defective item was a sofa. The tenant was awarded damages against the landlord. The landlord, however, was, in turn, able to sue the manufacturer of the sofa to recover what he, the landlord, was required to pay to the tenant.

The question is whether an item is really personal property or is affixed to the building in such a manner as to be considered a part of the building. See Section 660 of the Civil Code. If the defective item is a fixture, such as a wall heater, rather than an item of personal property, the above rule is not applicable.

Suppose a water pipe breaks and damage is sustained, not to tenant, but to his property. The rules pertaining to recovery for such damage are generally the same as the rules applicable to injury directly to the tenant. A broken water pipe would probably be considered a latent defect and ordinarily the landlord would not be liable.

Californians should take special note of drastic changes in the law relative to the liability of the landlord for injuries to a tenant.

Section 1714 of the Civil Code makes every person responsible for the injuries of another if the injury is caused by the lack of ordinary care in the maintenance of property.

37

The new trend in California and some other states is to hold the landlords responsible for injuries sustained by tenants where the landlord's negligence has created an unreasonable risk of harm. In California, the case of *Brennan vs. Cockrell* held that a landlord was liable to a tenant when the tenant fell because of a defective handrail.

In a later case a landlord was held liable to a guest of a tenant when the guest was bitten by a vicious dog which belonged to another tenant. Allowing the dog to remain on the property created an unreasonable risk to the tenants. The court held that the landlord could have gotten rid of the dog by getting rid of the dog's owner.

The courts are extending the law even further for the protection of tenants and others who come on the property. *Golden v. Conway* held that the landlord was responsible for injuries caused by a defective appliance he had installed even though he did not know the appliance was defective. In another case, the landlord failed to respond to requests to repair an electrical outlet. The tenant was forced to use an extension cord. The landlord was held responsible for fire damage caused by the defective cord even though the cord belonged to the tenant!

In still another case, *O'Hara v. Western Seven Trees*, a woman was raped and injured in an apartment building. The landlord was liable for her injuries. No, he wasn't the one who raped her, but he had failed to warn her when she moved in that there had been other rapes in the building. In addition, he had misrepresented to her the extent of the security features of the building.

Generally, a landlord may not "contact away" his liability. In other words if a lease provides that a landlord will not be liable for injuries sustained by a tenant (which were caused by the landlord's negligence) that provision will be invalid.

# CHAPTER SEVEN
## Forcible Entry, Forcible Detainer, And Eviction

Some of the most frequently asked questions by landlords and tenants are:

A. "The tenant won't pay his rent. Can I lock him out?"

B. "The landlord keeps coming in my apartment and threatening me. What can I do?"

The answers to these and other related questions will be discussed in this chapter.

Few landlords, and fewer tenants are aware of the provisions of the Forcible Entry and Detainer statutes. If you are a landlord you should certainly read this chapter, for an awareness of it's contents could prevent you from finding yourself on the losing end of an expensive lawsuit.

Tenants should carefully read on and take heed. If the landlord is guilty of conduct of such a nature as to be in violation of Sections 1159 and 1160 of the Code of Civil Procedure, a calm reading aloud of these sections to the landlord (or a showing of these pages to him) may cause an abrupt change in his behavior.

The Forcible Entry and Detainer laws were enacted to prevent violence and to protect tenants in the quiet and peaceful enjoyment of their dwellings.

It is suggested at this time that you turn to the Appendix and read Sections 1159 and 1160 of the Code of Civil Procedure.

Section 1159 defines a forcible entry. Notice that a forcible entry can be achieved in two ways. The entry can be by actual force. The entry is also considered to be by force if it is a peaceful entry which is followed by threats or menacing conduct. In the latter instance, the determination of what constitutes threats or menacing conduct would depend upon the facts of each case. A threat to bring a formal eviction action would probably not be considered strong enough for a court to award damages to a tenant. A threat to lock a tenant out or to cause him bodily harm would probably be sufficient even if the threat followed a peaceful entry.

Section 1160 would apply to situations where a landlord, for example, takes possession of an apartment in the absence of the tenant and refuses to allow the tenant to reenter. Notice that this section refers to "occupant" rather than tenant. This would indicate that a landlord would be guilty of a wrongdoing even if he took possession from the guest of a tenant.

The Forcible Entry and Detainer statutes apply in situations where a tenant, even though wrongfully in possession because of nonpayment of rent, is the victim of a breach of the peace. Situations in which a tenant is in rightful possession, but is wrongfully evicted will be discussed later.

A tenant in a Forcible Entry action must show:

A.   That he was in possession of the property. A temporary absence does not mean that a tenant is not in possession.

B.   That the landlord used force or violence, either before or after the entry.

Wrongful entry with a pass key in the absence of the tenant is sufficient to constitute a forcible entry. The changing of a lock by a landlord is also sufficient. Removal of the tenant's furniture by the landlord would constitute force and violence.

C.   That there was an entry. It can be in any of the ways already discussed or it can occur in a peaceful manner (if the peaceful entry is followed by force or violence).

It is doubtful that a provision in a lease or rental agreement in which a tenant consents to an entry by the landlord could avoid liability under the Forcible Entry and Detainer laws. A landlord would be assuming a great risk if he chose to rely on such a provision as an excuse for breaching the peace.

It is conceivable that a *landlord* could maintain an action for Forcible Entry and Detainer against a *tenant* if the tenant, once lawfully evicted, attempted to retake possession of the premises. The landlord, if he was successful in this case, could recover for damages to the premises and loss of rents occasioned by the tenant's wrongful entry.

Now let's discuss the situation where the tenant is rightfully on the premises and the landlord evicts him. If the eviction is not justified, the tenant can sue for wrongful eviction rather than for Forcible Entry.

What is the advantage of an eviction action over a Forcible Entry and Detainer action?

In a Forcible Entry and Detainer action, before the tenant can be given money damages by the court he must have the premises restored to him. In an eviction action, possession need not be restored to the tenant.

In addition, the allowable damages that can be awarded by a court in an eviction action are greater. In an eviction action the tenant can be awarded damages for inconvenience and mental anguish. He can also recover for any difference in increased rent that he might be required to pay in a new dwelling. In one California case a tenant was awarded damages for increased rent on his new apartment for the term of the lease of his new apartment even though he was only on a month to month agreement in the place from which he was evicted.

What is eviction?

Eviction can be actual or constructive. Actual eviction occurs where the tenant is physically ousted or is actually deprived of the possession of his dwelling. Locking a tenant out is an example of actual eviction.

Constructive eviction occurs where the premises are rendered unsuitable for occupancy. Examples of constructive eviction are: (a) violations of health laws in the maintenance of the premises and (b) harassment by the landlord.

In a 1968 case, *Conterno v. Brown*, a tenant was not allowed to bring an action for eviction where he claimed that the continuous noise of other tenants deprived him of the quiet enjoyment of his apartment. He lost the case because the lease provided that the landlord would not be liable for acts of other tenants. Another example of the importance of putting things in a lease or rental agreement.

The leading Forcible Entry and Detainer case is *Jordan v. Talbott*. In that case the landlord, in the tenant's absence, entered the apartment and removed the tenant's belongings. *Even though the lease had a provision for right of entry*, the court said that such a provision could not justify a breach of the peace. The tenant in that case was awarded $6500 damages. See the next chapter on the Baggage Lien Law. The new law permits the landlord to enter, even in the absence of the tenant, but only if he has a court order.

So, landlords beware! It may be hard to swallow, but if you want to evict a tenant, do it by complying with the notice requirements or by bringing an unlawful detainer action. Do not attempt an eviction by committing a breach of the peace.

And tenants, don't forget this chapter. If your landlord is harassing you, invite him in for a little reading from your trusty Landlord-Tenant manual and outsmart him psychologically.

# CHAPTER EIGHT
## The Baggage Lien Law

Tommy Tenant is two months behind in his rent. One day, Larry Landlord, without notice, comes in and removes Tommy Tenant's television set, clothes and other personal belongings. He refuses to return them until Tommy Tenant pays the rent. Larry Landlord doesn't know it, but he is in big trouble.

What is the Baggage Lien law? To begin with, it has little to do with baggage. It is a law which imposes a lien upon certain property of the tenant and allows landlord to hold and sell said property to recover overdue rent. More importantly, it is a law which limits the manner by which a landlord can take a tenant's property to satisfy the nonpayment of rent.

The law is found in Section 1861a of the Civil Code. You will readily see that the statute does not permit the lien to apply to much of the tenant's property. Most household furniture and appliances are immune from the lien.

A landlord cannot simply enter a tenant's abode and remove his property to satisy unpaid rent. There are numerous prerequisites which must be met before the property may be taken. They are:

A.   A lawsuit must be filed for rents due; and

B.   A court order must be obtained to permit entry into the apartment; and

C.   A bond must be posted with the court.

Prior to the enactment of this law, a landlord would be liable for damages under the Forcible Entry and Detainer law even if he entered the tenant's apartment with a pass key. (Remember *Jordan v. Talbott* in Chapter 7?) Now, however, if the court order is first obtained, the landlord will not be liable for damages if he enters with a pass key in a peaceful manner and removes the property during daylight hours.

After the landlord wins his lawsuit for rent, he may, if the tenant does not pay the judgment within 30 days, sell the property. He must, however, give 15 days' notice and sell the property at public auction.

As you can see, the Baggage Lien law is expensive and complicated to enforce and reaches very little property.

Landlords must be extremely careful not to take property without a court order. Failure to first obtain a court order could render a landlord liable for conversion. That means that even if the landlord later decides to return the property, he may be liable for damages to the tenant for whatever the fair market value of the property was at the time he, the landlord, appropriated it.

The law seems to be more useful to tenants to convince a landlord that he cannot just come in and take a tenant's property. Next time a landlord just walks in and takes your property for nonpayment of rent, a reading of 1861a should result in the rapid return of your property.

So remember, landlords, if you want to take the tenant's property under the Baggage Lien law, be sure you comply with the following checklist:

A.   Sue for the correct amount of unpaid rent;

B.   Obtain a court order to remove the property;

C.   Enter during the daytime hours and do so only if you will not be met with resistance;

D.   Make certain that the property you take is not exempt under the statute;

E.   Obtain a judgment, that is, complete your case against the tenant in court; and

F.   Comply with the statute relative to notice and public sale.

For methods of acquiring property of an abandoned tenant, see Chapter 10.

# CHAPTER NINE
## Unlawful Detainer And Other Unpleasant
## Ways To Terminate A Tenancy

Unlawful detainer is the method by which a landlord obtains the assistance of the court to remove a tenant.

The remedy of unlawful detainer is one available to landlords in five situations:

1. Where the tenant continues in possession of the property after the lease expires;

2. Where the tenant continues in possession of the property after failure to perform certain conditions or covenants of the lease;

3. Where the tenant continues in possession after a default in rent;

4. Where the tenant commits waste or a nuisance upon the premises or uses the premises for an unlawful purpose, or wrongfully assigns or sublets the premises; and

5. Where a tenant gives a written notice of intention to terminate a tenancy or where the parties agree upon a termination date and the tenant fails to deliver possession on that date.

See Code of Civil Procedure Section 1161.

A landlord may bring an unlawful detainer action even though he has taken security in the form of a chattel mortgage or under the Baggage Lien Law.

Since the remedy of unlawful detainer is what is referred to as "summary in nature", that is, the court is asked to move swiftly in ousting the tenant, the duty of the landlord to comply with the requisites necessary to compel the court to act is strictly enforced.

To have a court remove a tenant, a landlord must file with the court a document known as a "complaint." A copy of a complaint, along with a summons must then be served on the tenant. After five days from receipt of the summons and complaint, the tenant must file a formal document with the court which is known as an "answer." The court will then schedule a hearing and determine whether the tenant should be removed from the property. If the tenant does not file the answer in the five day period, he is said to have "defaulted" and the court, in his absence, will award the premises to the landlord.

The court has the power in certain cases to award immediate possession of the premises to the landlord. The courts can oust the tenant even before the five day period to answer the complaint has expired. If the tenant has concealed himself or has left the state or cannot be found, the court may award immediate possession to the landlord.

There are many, many technical defenses which a tenant might have to an unlawful detainer action. It is, therefore, unlikely that either a landlord or a tenant could successfully act as his own attorney in an unlawful detainer action. The rules and procedures are highly technical and failure to follow them can prove costly.

The primary aim of this chapter, therefore, is to enlighten the reader as to what is involved. An informed client is an easier client for an attorney to work with and it is hopeful that the information which can be gained through this chapter would create a better understanding between the reader and his attorney.

For an example of a summons and complaint in an unlawful detainer action, see the Appendix.

It is always to the landlord's advantage if he can avoid an unlawful detainer action. The attorney's fees are usually around $200, court costs about $25, and the cost of removal of the tenant around $200. The cost of removal is determined by the number of rooms in the premises. The sheriff, who must hire a moving van to remove and store the tenant's property, charges approximately $50 per room. A four room apartment, therefore, results in a cost of approximately $200. The total cost, therefore, is approximately $400 to $500.

Since the cost of an unlawful detainer action is so expensive, it is often more practical to find another method of removing a squatting tenant who won't pay his rent.

One method would be to sue the tenant each month in small claims court as his rent becomes due. Then, after acquiring a judgment, the tenant's wages or property can be attached. A few months of this and a tenant might grow weary and either move or pay his rent. This method is effective, of course, only if the tenant has a job or has property which can be attached.

Sometimes the mere bringing of an unlawful detainer action is enough to frighten a tenant. The sheriff, in uniform, appearing at the door with the summons and complaint shows that the landlord means business. The tenant, not desiring to be involved with the law, may quickly move.

The quickest and most effective method which the author himself has used is to offer the tenant $100 cash upon condition, and *after* he removes himself. This is a severe blow to the pride, but easier on the pocket book in the long run when one considers the expense of an unlawful detainer action (not to mention the cost suffered by a continued loss of rent).

It is true that the lost rent and/or expenses of an unlawful detainer action can be recovered from a tenant after he moves, but as a practical matter a tenant who was unable to pay his rent certainly would not be able to afford these additional costs.

Section 1174 of the Code of Civil Procedure does provide that a landlord may keep and store personal property which the tenant has abandoned and hold it for payment of the costs incurred in the unlawful detainer action. The section does not seem to limit the property that can be taken. The section does not contain the exclusions which one finds so restrictive in the Baggage Lien Law.

The section also provides for a method of selling the property after a lapse of 30 days. Refer to Section 1174 in the Appendix.

On January 1, 1976 CCP Section 1174 will be amended to provide for a remedy wherein the landlord can dispose of abandoned property after an eviction. The remedies are similar to those described in Chapter 10.

How are the wheels of an unlawful detainer action put into motion?

A notice to quit is required in most cases before an unlawful detainer action can be filed. And remember, the notice must strictly comply with the requirements of the law. An example of a notice to quit or pay rent is included in the Appendix.

The notice, in the case of nonpayment of rent, must demand either the rent or possession of the property.

In the case of the failure to perform a condition or a convenant, the notice must describe the condition or covenant which has not been performed and that the failure to perform it will result in the landlord seeking possession.

The notice must be *either*:

1.   Personally served on the tenant; or

2. Left with a person of suitable age either at tenant's residence or place of business, if tenant can't be found, and by mailing a copy to tenant at his place of residence; or

3. Posting on the leased property in a conspicuous place (if no one can be found there) and mailing a copy to the tenant's residence.

A landlord must make an election in his notice whether to declare a forfeiture of the lease. If he declares a forfeiture, he cannot sue for future rent. Declaring a forfeiture also deprives a tenant of the right to pay the back rent after judgment and have the premises restored. If the landlord does not declare a forfeiture, the tenant, after judgment, has 5 days to pay the back rent, plus costs, and have the premises restored to him. The advantage in not declaring a forfeiture is that if the tenant does not have the premises restored to him, the obligation of the tenant to pay future rent continues even though he no longer has possession of the premises.

The notice should also indicate that the landlord intends to seek treble damages. This alone may be enough to frighten a tenant to give up possession.

The notice must allow at least three days for the tenant to cure the default. The days are counted by omitting the first and including the last. For example, if the notice is served on January 1, the third day would fall on January 4, unless that day is a holiday. On January 5 landlord could file his summons and complaint with the court.

The notice must demand the exact amount of rent due. It can demand less, but if it demands more, the notice is defective.

Suppose the tenant's rent is $100 per month. Suppose his rent is due on the first of each month and he did not pay on January 1 or on February 1. On February 2, the landlord could demand $200, since the landlord is not required to apportion the rent.

If the tenant gets landlord to accept a portion of the $200 after the service of the notice, the lessor cannot thereafter bring his action but must start all over again with a new notice. This is a good tenant tip; if the tenant can get the landlord to accept $25, for example, the landlord's whole case is frustrated and he must start all over again. Then, after the landlord serves a new notice, try to get him to accept another $25.

But here is a good landlord tip. Suppose the tenant is two months behind. Suppose the rent is $100 per month. If you know that the tenant can come up with only $100, give him a notice to quit in which you demand only $100. Then, after he pays the $100, give him another notice for the remaining $100. Since he won't be able to pay it, you can have him evicted.

If the landlord holds a security deposit, he can still bring an unlawful detainer action, but if he holds a first and last months' rent, he must give credit for the last month's rent in his notice to quit. If he doesn't the notice will be defective.

So, in our above example, if the tenant had previously paid the first and last months' rent, then on February 1 he would only owe $100 even though he was obligated to pay $200 by February 1. The notice to quit should in this case only demand $100.

Where an unlawful detainer action is being brought after a lease has expired or after a property was supposed to be vacated, no three day notice is required. But suppose a landlord desires to end a month to month tenancy. Before he can bring an unlawful detainer action, he must show that he previously gave a 30 day notice to quit (or a 7 day notice if the month to month agreement so provided). If either the 30 day or 7 day notice was given, no further notice is required.

In an unlawful detainer situation, if a tenant can establish that the premises are in a state of disrepair and in violation of the housing code, such facts can constitute a defense. The court will deduct from the rent the damage incurred by the tenant because of the defects. The courts now say that when a landlord rents a dwelling he is given an implied warranty that the premises are in a habitable condition. What usually happens is that the court allows the tenant to remain in the dwelling at a reduced rent. *Green vs. Superior Court.*

Two additional methods of terminating a lease or rental agreement are by surrender or abandonment.

A surrender is accomplished when a tenant vacates the premises and the landlord agrees to relieve the tenant from any further obligations under the lease or rental agreement.

An abandonment is a voluntary relinquishment of the property, not necessarily to the landlord, but to any one who might retake the property. Abandonment consists of:

A. Voluntarily leaving the premises vacant and unoccupied; and

B. The intention not to return.

There are several new statutes which deal with a landlord's rights when a tenant breaches or abandons a lease.

Section 1951.2 of the Civil Code sets out the amount of damages which the landlord may recover. Some of the computations are rather complex.

Briefly, the landlord is entitled to the amount of the rent past due, plus interest at a rate stated in the lease, or, if not stated, then at the legal rate.

The landlord is also entitled to the reasonable value of the future rent which the tenant would have paid had he remained as a tenant. The tenant is entitled to an offset for the amount of rent which the landlord could have acquired had the landlord made reasonable efforts to re-rent the property. The tenant is, of course, also entitled to a credit for the rents which the landlord did, in fact, obtain after the tenant's abandonment.

The proper language to include in a lease for a landlord or tenant to insure his rights under Section 1951.2 can be found in paragraph IX of Chapter 2.

Section 1951.4 of the Civil Code allows the landlord to keep the property vacant and sue the tenant as the rent becomes due each month. But this section is available to landlords only if the lease reserved to the tenant the right to assign or sublet. See paragraph X of Chapter 2.

In abandonment situations, a landlord must be careful not to accept the surrender of the premises. Such a surrender will terminate the tenant's obligation. If you inform the tenant that you are reentering the premises only to re-rent for the owner's benefit, you can avoid this pitfall.

A lease can be rescinded by either party for a variety of other reasons. Rescission is a legal action by which the court orders the termination of the lease.

If either party can establish that the other fraudulently induced him to enter into the lease agreement, the aggrieved party might petition the court to cancel (i.e., rescind) the lease.

If the landlord deprives the tenant of his right to quiet enjoyment, the tenant may have grounds to rescind the lease. Of course, the landlord may be harassing the tenant for the very purpose of provoking the tenant to try and rescind the lease.

A lease will be automatically terminated by the total destruction of the property or if the property is taken by the government under its right of eminent domain.

Where the property is only partially destroyed or where the government takes only a portion of the property, the lease is not automatically terminated. Tenants, therefore, should spell out in the lease that a partial destruction or partial condemnation will terminate the lease. See paragraph XXX in Chapter 2.

Death of the tenant, bankruptcy of the tenant, or a sale of the property does not automatically terminate the lease. As with any other contingency, spell it out if you want it to operate as a means of terminating the lease.

Incidentally, landlords, one way *not* to terminate a tenancy is by the turning off of the utilities.

Civil Code Section 789.3, enacted in 1972, frowns on such conduct. A landlord who, with the intent of terminating the tenancy, shuts off the utilities is liable to the tenant for damages, plus $100 for each day the tenant is deprived of his utilities, plus attorney's fees.

So forget about turning off the tenant's utilities as a method of getting him out.

If a lease has been terminated under Section 1951.2 (see page 49) and the tenant has notified the landlord in writing that he, the tenant wants notice of what happend to any advance rental payments, a written notice must be given to the tenant stating the name and address of the new tenant and the length of the new lease. The notice must be sent within 30 days of the start of the new lease. It may be delivered personally or sent by regular mail. The notice is not required if the advance rental payment does not exceed one month or if the amount of due and unpaid rent exceeds the amount of the advance.

# CHAPTER TEN
## What To Do When the Tenant Flies the Coop

Expecting a check from Tommy Tenant, Larry Landlord goes to his mailbox on the first of the month. No check. Not even a postcard. Follow-up trips to the box produce only bills. A week or so later Larry sojourns to Tommy's apartment. He looks through the window (a peeping Larry) and sees an apartment virtually empty except for a stereo and a few letters demanding that it be paid for. What can Larry do?

A reasonable man would conclude that Tommy has abandoned his apartment. Abandonment raises so many unique problems that the California legislature has seen fit to enact some new laws to answer some of these questions.

A lessor can enter a tenant's property without complying with the unlawful detainer statutes only when the tenant has abandoned the property and has thereby lost his right to possession. *Kassan vs. Stout*, 9 Cal. 3rd 39. The question is, what constitutes an abandonment?

A new law, Section 1951.3 of the Civil Code answers this question.

Property shall be deemed abandoned and the lease shall terminate if the lessor gives notice in writing of his belief of abandonment and the lessee fails to give written notice of his intention not to abandon, and if he fails to give notice of his address where he can be served with an unlawful detainer action.

The lessor can give notice of his belief only after the rent has been due and unpaid for at least 14 consecutive days and the lessor reasonably believes that the tenant has in fact abandoned. The date of termination should be specified in the lessor's notice and shall be no less than 15 days after the notice is personally served or, if mailed, not less than 18 days after the notice is deposited in the mail.

The notice shall be delivered personally or by first class mail to lessee's last known address, plus at any other address where the lessor reasonably believes the lessee will receive it.

The notice shall be in substantially the following form:

## Notice of Belief of Abandonment

To _____
(Name of lessee/tenant)

_____
(Address of lessee/tenant)

This notice is given pursuant to Section 1951.3 of the Civil Code concerning the real property leased by you at _____ (state location of the property by address or other sufficient description). The rent on this propery has been due and unpaid for 14 consecutive days and the lessor/landlord believes that you have abandoned the property.

The real property will be deemed abandoned within the meaning of Section 1951.2 of the Civil Code and your lease will terminate on _____ (here insert a date not less than 15 days after this notice is served personally or, if mailed, not less than 18 days after this notice is deposited in the mail) unless before such date the undersigned receives at the address indicated below a written notice from you stating both of the following:

(1) Your intent not to abandon the real property.

(2) An address at which you may be served by certified mail in any action for unlawful detainer of the real property.

You are required to pay the rent due and unpaid on this real property as required by the lease, and your failure to do so can lead to a court proceeding against you.

Dated: _____      _____
(Signature of lessor/landlord)

_____
(Type or print name of lessor/landlord)

_____
(Address to which lessee/tenant is to send notice)

The lessee can establish that there was no abandonment if he can (1) prove that the rent was not due and unpaid for 14 days; or (2) that the lessor did not have a reasonable belief that the property was abandoned; or (3) that, prior to the date specified in lessor's notice, lessee stated his intent not to abandon; or (4) the lessee, within the above date specified, pays the rent due.

The lessor can still proceed with an unlawful detainer action if the rent is not paid.

For remedies of lessor with respect to a suit for unpaid rent, see CC Section 1951.4 in the appendix. Remember that efforts to re-rent the property to mitigate the lessee's damages do not relieve the lessee of the obligation to pay rent.

What happens to personal property remaining on the premises after the tenant vacates? Sections 1980-1990 are new and deal with this problem.

The notice shall adequately describe the property except that locked boxes, etc. may be described without describing their contents. The notice shall state that reasonable charges shall be made for storage. The notice shall state where and before what date the property may be claimed. The date shall be not less than 15 days from personal service of the notice or 18 days from mailing. If mailed, it must be sent first class to the last known address, plus to the vacated premises. A copy must also be sent to any other person who might own the property.

The notice must be in the following form:

### Notice of Right to Reclaim Abandoned Property

To: _____
(Name of former tenant)

_____
(Address of former tenant)

When you vacated the premises at _____

_____(address of premises, including room or apartment number, if any)the following personal property remained:

_____
(insert description of the personal property)

You may claim this property at _____

_____(address where property may be claimed.) Unless you pay the reasonable cost of storage for all the above-described property, and take possession of the property which you claim, not later than _____(insert date not less than 15 days after notice is personally delivered or, if mailed, not less than 18 days after notice is deposited in the mail) this property may be disposed of pursuant to Civil Code Section 1988.

(Insert here the statement required by subdivision (b) of this section)

Dated: _____        _____

(Signature of landlord)

_____
(Type or print name of landlord)

_____
(Telephone number)

_____
(Address)

The notice must also contain one of the following statements:

(1) If you fail to reclaim the property, it will be sold at a public sale after notice of the sale has been given by publication. You have the right to bid on the property at this sale. After the property is sold and is deducted, the remaining money will be paid over to the county. You may claim the remaining money at any time within one year after the county receives the money."

(2) Because this property is believed to be worth less than $100, it may be kept, sold, or destroyed without further notice if you fail to reclaim it within the time indicated above."

A notice to any other person whom the lessor reasonably believes to be the owner should be in the following form:

Notice of Right to Reclaim Abandoned Property

To: _____
(Name)

_____
(Address)

When _____
(name of former tenant)

vacated the premises at _____
(address of premises, including room or

apartment number, if any)
the following personal property remained: _____
(insert description of the

_____
personal property)
If you own any of this property, you may claim it at _____
(address where

_____
property may be claimed)
Unless you pay the reasonable cost of storage and take possession of the property to which you are entitled not later than _____ (insert date not less than 15 days after notice is personally delivered or, if mailed, not less than 18 days after notice is deposited in the mail) this property may be disposed of pursuant to Civil Code Section 1988.

Dated: _____     _____
(Signature of landlord)

_____
(Type or print name of landlord)

_____
(Telephone number)

_____
(Address)

54

The landlord must use reasonable care in storing the property. The landlord must release the property to the tenant or other person if demand is made and storage costs are paid within the time limit in the notice. If sold at public sale it must be released to the tenant if he claims it prior to sale and pays costs of storage, sale and advertising.

If the property is to be sold and is worth less than $100, the landlord may retain it. Otherwise, the notice of sale must be published in a newspaper. All proceeds in excess of costs must be deposited with the county. The tenant may claim the excess within one year.

Landlords must be careful in releasing property to third persons. If a landlord releases property to a person who, through reasonable investigation, could have been determined to be not the rightful owner, the landlord could be liable to the tenant for the value of the property.

# CHAPTER ELEVEN
## Retaliatory Eviction

What is retaliatory eviction? It is a relatively new concept in the law. It provides a tenant with ammunition against a landlord when the landlord has attempted to evict the tenant for no reason other than to get back at him. When a landlord tries to evict a tenant or raise his rent only because the tenant has demanded that his premises be put in a livable condition, the law will step in to assist the tenant. This assistance is called the defense of Retaliatory Eviction. Retaliatory Eviction is to eviction as self defense is to murder.

The situation which usually gives rise to a retaliatory eviction is one in which the tenant demands that repairs be made under Section 1941 of the Civil Code (See Chapter 5) or in which the tenant reports the landlord for some violation of a local building or health ordinance.

In a 1970 California case, entitled *Schweiger v. Supreme Court*, a month to month tenant requested the landlord to repair two broken windows. The landlord refused. The tenant informed the landlord that he, the tenant, would repair the windows and deduct the cost from the rent pursuant to his right under Civil Code Section 1942. The landlord responded by giving the tenant a 30 day notice to raise the rent from $75.00 to $125.00. The tenant refused to pay the increase and the landlord sued to evict him. The court held that the landlord's only motive in raising the rent and attempting to evict the tenant for failure to pay the raised rent was to retaliate for the tenant's asserting his lawful right to insist that the dwelling be made tenantable. The court, therefore, refused to evict the tenant under the circumstances.

The California legislature, in 1971, enacted Civil Code Section 1942.5 as a result of the above case. The section is set forth in the Appendix. It says in effect that if a landlord has, as his dominant purpose, retaliation against the tenant because the tenant either attempts to exercise his right under Section 1942 of the Civil Code or because the tenant complained to a governmental agency about the tenantability of the dwelling, the landlord may not in retaliation, recover possession of the dwelling unless the tenant is in default in the payment of rent.

There are two additional limitations to this section:

A. The eviction will be considered retaliatory only if the landlord attempts to evict the tenant within 60 days from the date that the tenant notified the landlord or the governmental agency of the defect in the premises, and

B.  A tenant may invoke the provision of 1942.5 only once in any 12 month period.

Subsection (d) of Section 1942.5 allows a landlord to terminate a tenancy if he notifies the tenant of the reasons for his action and the reasons are bona fide and are not retaliatory. In this case the landlord can still evict the tenant even if the tenant had theretofore attempted to have repairs made or if the tenant had previously reported the landlord to a governmental agency for defects in the property.

A word of caution to the tenant — the 60 day period begins from the time a written complaint is filed with a governmental agency or the date of inspection by the agency, whichever is later. Therefore, it would appear that a written complaint is necessary if the tenant wants to be protected under this section.

Tenants cannot waive their rights under the retaliatory eviction statute by any agreement in the lease. Such an agreement would be void and against public policy.

There are no statutes relating to retaliatory eviction or any other act of the tenant, such as organizing other tenants, going on welfare, or wearing hair too long. The trend in Supreme Court cases, however, especially those involving racial discrimination, is to forbid arbitrary eviction on any such grounds.

In conclusion, retaliatory eviction is not a method by which a tenant can get money damages. It is designed solely as a way of preventing an eviction in the limited situation stated in Section 1942.5 of the Civil Code.

# CHAPTER 12
## State and Local Labor and Housing Laws

Landlords should be keenly aware of their obligations under the State Public Housekeeping Law. If your apartment building contains three or more units, you fall under its provisions. Many landlords have sorrowfully discovered too late that managers of apartment buildings must be paid a minimum wage. (There is no Federal minimum wage requirement unless the gross rentals exceed $250,000 annually, or unless the employees are handling products used in interstate commerce.

The author on several occasions has represented landlords who, a year or so after dismissing a manager, found themselves faced with a lawsuit for thousands of dollars. Some people have been known to obtain managerial positions with the premeditated intent of working for a period, quitting, and then suing for back wages.

An owner of an apartment building must pay a manager a minimum of $2.75 per hour, plus time and a half for over 40 hours a week. The landlord is allowed a credit against the manager's wages for the manager's use of an apartment of no more than $115 per month.

The landlord is required to maintain records showing the name and age of the manager, the hours which the manager worked and the total wages paid.

Suppose a manager is required to keep himself available to show apartments to prospective tenants during an entire weekend. Even though the manager is engaged on other activities of his own while he is awating prospective tenants, he is entitle to compensation for the entire period during which he is required to keep himself available.

The situation frequently arises in which a landlord hires a husband and wife to act as co-managers. It is often hard to determine who is putting in the hours, the husband or the wife. Frequently the wife will put in a claim for wages long after she and her husband have quit. The landlord, if he kept no records, is in a poor position to establish that the women's claim is a false one.

To avoid this, it is strongly advised that a landlord require the manager to sign a time card every day so that if later he decides to bring an action against the landlord, the landlord will have proof as to exactly how many hours he worked.

It is not possible to relate in this book all the complicated rules which are set forth in the Wage and Hour Law. Every apartment owner who employs a female manager should acquire a copy of the law from the Division of Industrial Welfare of his state and thoroughly familiarize himself with the provisions of that law. Not only can non-compliance with the law result in extraordinary pecuniary loss to the landlord but willful violations are considered misdemeanors and are punishable by fine or jail.

Here are several other aspects of the labor laws with which you should be familiar.

A resident manager must be employed in buildings of 16 or more units if the owner does not live on the premises. In buildings of 4 or more units, the name, address and telephone number of an absentee owner must be posted in a conspicuous place.

Wages must be paid immediately when an employee is terminated. They must be paid within 48 hours if an employee quits. If not paid within these times, an employee can sue the employer for his daily wage for an additional 30 day period, or until paid, whichever occurs first. Labor Code Section 201.

Payment of wages with a bad check is a misdemeanor. A conviction can be punished by the imposition of a fine of $500 and/or imprisonment for up to 6 months.

An employee, in a suit for wages, can recover attorney's fees in an amount up to 20% of the recovery.

Persons employed by landlords come under the laws requiring the withholding of funds for federal income tax, state unemployment taxes and workmen's compensation insurance. These requirements apply to all employees except "casual" employees. Casual employees or independent contractors are excluded. To determine whether an individual is a casual employee or an independent contractor, factors considered are the control exercised by the employer, the type of occupation, whether the employer furnishes the tools of the occupation, and the method of payment.

When in doubt it is always advisable to get an opinion from the Labor Commission or the Internal Revenue Service. Failure to comply can result in severe penalties.

Many states and cities have regulations covering building and sanitary laws. Landlords should familiarize themselves with these laws for a number of reasons. For one, failure to comply can result in the loss or denial of a license to rent your units. In addition, a violation can enable a tenant to legally avoid payment of rent. See Chapter 5.

The State Housing law in California is governed by the Department of Housing and Community Development. In addition, most cities have their own rules. Both agencies should be consulted for a list of their requirements.

# CHAPTER 13
## Fair Housing Laws

In the past decade, most states have enacted laws which prohibit discriminatory renting of dwellings on the basis of race, color, creed, religion, ancestry or national origin.

In addition, the Federal Government, in 1964, enacted the Federal Civil Rights Act. This act applies to all states.

The Federal Fair Housing Law prohibits discrimination in any federally assisted housing project. The following types of housing, even if not federally assisted, that is, not financed by federal funds, are also covered under the law: Multifamily dwellings of five or more units; multifamily dwellings of up to four units if the owner does not live on the premises; single family dwellings not owned by a private individual; single family dwellings owned by a private person who owned more than three such houses at the same time or who sells more than one such house within any two years in which he was not the most recent occupant prior to sale or any house sold or rented through a broker.

California enacted the Unruh Civil Rights Act which, in effect, carries the same force as the Federal law. One who violates the Unruh Act can be held liable for civil damages. In addition, a violation constitutes a misdemeanor. Civil Code Section 51 provides for damages in the amount of $250. The Unruh Act applies only to business activities, but a 1962 case held that an owner of a triplex was operating a business. A 1971 case, *Flowers vs. Burnham*, held that discrimination against a family with children under five years of age did not constitute a violation.

The Rumford Fair Housing Law was enacted in 1963. In addition to applying to businesses under the Unruh Act, it extends to all housing of five or more units. Enforcement is under the Fair Employment Practices Commission. Complaints must be filed within 60 days of the violation. The commission can require the guilty party to rent the unit to the complaining party, or rent similar accommodations, or pay damages up to $500.

It is a violation to refuse to rent to blind persons because they require the services of a seeing eye dog. It is also a violation to refuse to rent to deaf persons. C.C. § 54.1.

# CHAPTER 14
## Condominiums and Cooperatives

There is often confusion about the difference between a condominium and a cooperative apartment.

A condominium is actually ownership in real property. It differs little from ownership in a single family dwelling. A condominium owner owns an individual interest in the condominium project plus a separate interest in a portion of the space within the project such as an apartment and a garage. He owns exclusively the area within his specific apartment. He owns an individual interest in common in the other areas such as the halls, grounds, pool, etc. He also has the right to sell, lease, or encumber (mortgage) his portion. See Civil Code Section 783.

Special care must be taken when one purchases a condominium. The condominium project must comply with the applicable statutes. A survey map must be recorded with the country recorder. In addition, diagrammatic floor plans with specific dimensions and locations must be made. The names of all record owners and lien-holders must be recorded.

A Declaration of Restrictions must be prepared for each project. It includes procedures for maintenance and management of the project. In short, a person purchasing a condominium agrees to be bound by the provisions and rules contained in the declaration. It is very important to study this document thoroughly before purchasing a condominium.

In a cooperative apartment house, the occupants do not own an interest in the land and/or portion of the building. They merely own stock in the corporation that owns the project. Ownership of the stock entitles the shareholder to a long term lease in the project. Shareholders are considered tenants and may be removed by unlawful detainer. The corporation is governed by a board of directors elected by the tenants.

Cooperatives can be dangerous investments in that the shareholder is at the mercy of the corporation. If the corporation fails to pay taxes or mortgage payments, the creditors could foreclose against the interest of the shareholder.

There are variations of the "own-your-own" apartment concept. Most of them have the disadvantage that abides with any enterprise where you can't select or have control over your partners. Of the various types, condominiums appear to be the safest and most practical alternative.

# CHAPTER 15
## Mobilehomes

The tremendous increase in the use of mobilehomes as dwellings has brought about much legislation.

A "Mobilehome Accommodation Structure" is defined as a building or structure which is designed to accommodate mobilehomes above grade level.

A "mobilehome" is a vehicle designed and equipped to contain not more than two dwelling units to be used without a permanent foundation.

Section 10850 of the Health and Safety Code sets forth the requirements of a mobilehome for purposes of habitability.

Briefly, a mobilehome must comply with Housing Code and Vehicle Code requirements. It must be structurally sound and protect the occupants from the elements. It must not be permanently attached to the ground.

A landlord must give a tenant 60 days written notice to remove his mobilehome from the park. It applies only to mobilehomes which are required to be removed under permit.

Tenancy in a mobilehome park can be terminated only for the following reasons:

1.  Failure of a tenant to comply with local or state mobilehome laws;

2.  Conduct of a tenant which constitutes an annoyance to other tenants or interference with park management;

3.  Failure to comply with rules of the park as established in the rental agreement, or as amended with the consent of the tenant, or without his consent upon six months written notice;

4.  Nonpayment of rent, utility charges, or reasonable service charges;

5.  Condemnation or changes in use of the park.

Notice of termination must state the specific reasons and facts for the termination.

No entry fee can be charged as a condition of entry or a selling fee as a condition of sale unless the management participates in the sale.

The recreation hall should be available for meetings of tenants to discuss park affairs at reasonable hours when the hall is not otherwise in use.

The management is required to furnish the tenant with a copy of the above laws.

Section 789.10 states that an owner of a mobilehome park cannot require a tenant to agree to move if the park is sold.

However, the owner can require:

1.    That mobilehomes less than 10 feet wide or over 10 years old or in a rundown condition may be removed;

2.    The right to approve the purchaser of a mobilehome of an existing tenant;

3.    That the above restrictions need not apply if a mobilehome is vacant more than 120 days.

Furthermore, before a mobile park owner can show a mobilehome to a new tenant or buyer, he must obtain written consent from the existing tenant.

A landlord must give 60 days' written notice of a rent increase. A tenant must give 60 days' notice of his intent to vacate a mobilehome.

Effective January 1, 1978, the owner of the park must give the tenant a written rental agreement listing the facilities and services to be provided and the responsibility of the owner to maintain the park.

In addition, the owner must agree in writing to meet with the tenants, on ten days' written notice, to discuss changes, amendments to rules, and deletion of services.

# CHAPTER 16
## The Small Claims Court

The small claims court is the arena in which battles are frequently fought by landlords and tenants.

It is an informal court where most of the usual complicated rules of procedure and evidence are relaxed.

The plaintiff is the person who is suing someone. The defendant is the person being sued.

Before you choose to sue someone in small claims court, take heed of this: The plaintiff has no right of appeal. This means that if the plaintiff loses in small claims court there is nothing he can do about it. The defendant, on the other hand, if he loses, can appeal to the superior court and get a new trial.

The small claims court has kept up with the trend of inflation. A few years ago the most you could sue for in the small claims court was $100. In 1972, after several increases, the limit was raised to $500.

The small claims court provides a person with a speedy and fair avenue of suing for money which he claims to be due to him. No lawyer is required to assist either party to the case. Indeed, lawyers are not even permitted in the small claims court.

How does one start a lawsuit in the small claims court?

First, you must determine where the suit must be filed. A telephone call to the clerk of the small claims court will quickly bring an answer to this. Generally, the case must be filed in the district either where the contract (lease or rental agreement) was made or where the defendant resides. So if you, as a landlord, own an apartment in Pasadena, for example, and the lease was made and payable there, and the tenant, after he moves out, resides in Los Angeles, either Pasadena or Los Angeles would be the proper place to start the lawsuit.

The suit is filed by making out a sworn statement setting forth the facts upon which you base your claim. The form for this is provided by the small claims clerk. You must appear personally to obtain and fill out these forms.

As we have stated, your claim cannot exceed $500. A claim cannot be split to avoid this limitation. Thus, if a tenant owes you $200 for rent and $400 for damage to furniture, you cannot file one lawsuit for the rent and another for the damages to the furniture. You may file only one lawsuit for $750 and, if you are successful, you will collect $400 for the rent and $350 for the damage to the furniture. You have, in effect, "waived the excess $50."

After the suit is filed, the court can authorize the papers to be mailed to the defendant, or the court can require the papers to be personally served.

The papers will contain a copy of your sworn statement, together with notification of the trial date.

The defendant may file a counterclaim against the plaintiff. He must serve the counterclaim on the plaintiff at least 5 days before the hearing. If defendant is served less than 10 days before the hearing, he must serve his counterclaim at least one day before the hearing.

When the case comes up for trial, each side will have an opportunity to tell his story to the judge. It is usually quite informal. If you have any witnesses, you must bring them into court. Don't rely on sworn statements or letters they have given you in place of their personal appearance. They must be present to testify. The court will not consider their hearsay statements, even if the statements are written and notarized.

If the defendant loses, he may appeal and obtain a new trial in the superior court. He may not appeal the counterclaim. If he did not appear in the small claims court, he must, within 20 days after receiving notice of a ruling aginst him, file a motion in the small claims court to vacate the ruling which was made against him.

Collecting a judgment is usually more difficult than obtaining one. The judgment cannot be enforced for 10 days. If defendant appeals, the judgment cannot be enforced until the appeal is decided. You may ask the clerk for an Abstract of Judgment. This means that if defendant owns or buys any real estate in the county, your judgment will be a lien. He can't sell the property until he pays you.

Another method of enforcement is to execute the wages, automobile, or other personal property of the defendant. Once you have located the property, go back to the clerk's office and the clerk will give you a "Writ of Execution." This writ is then taken to the Marshal (who is usually in the same building) and he goes to the defendant's employer and executes on the defendant's wages or picks up his car or boat or whatever you direct him to seize (except furniture, clothing and most personal effects which are exempt from execution).

So, good luck in the small claims court. It's a good place to seek justice, to see how the law functions, but most important, it's a good place to get a grievance off your chest and have your day in court.

# EPILOGUE

Well, have you acquired some new smarts with which to outsmart your landlord (if you're a tenant) or your tenant (if you're a landlord)?

Wouldn't it be better if you would never have to be involved with unlawful detainers, baggage liens, forcible entries or any of that ugly stuff?

Perhaps you won't have to. Perhaps, armed with your recently obtained knowledge, you can approach your adversary and say, "Look, let's *not* be adversaries. I know what the law is and the law will assist me if I need it. But let's try and settle our differences without the law."

It has often been said that the only ones who profit from a lawsuit are the lawyers. No one else ever wins. The expense, the aggravation and the consumption of time frequently usurp all of the profits of the victory.

So try to be friends, try and get along, enjoy your castle (if you're a tenant), love your tenant (if you're a landlord) and above all . . . live in peace.

# QUESTIONS AND ANSWERS

Q. Is it necessary to obtain a license to operate an apartment building?

A. It depends upon the city in which your building is located. Los Angeles, for instance, requires a license for buildings with three or more units. The city clerk of your city can answer the question for you.

Q. Must a lease be signed by the landlord and the tenant?

A. If the landlord signs the lease, it will be binding on the tenant if the tenant takes possession and pays the rent, even in the absence of his signature. Tenants should sign, however, so that there will be no dispute that they were unaware of the terms of the lease. Wives of the landlord and tenant should also sign. See Chapter 2.

Q. Can I refuse to rent to individuals of certain racial groups?

A. No. A refusal could result in a suit for damages.

Q. Can I refuse to rent to individuals with children or pets?

A. Yes, but don't be surprised if your right to refuse will some day be restricted by the legislature or the courts.

Q. Can I insist upon the payment of the rent if it falls due on a Sunday or a holiday?

A. No. But a tenant may, if he desires, pay the rent if it falls due on a Sunday or holiday.

Q. How soon must I sue for back rent?

The law governing the time limit during which a suit may be instituted is called the Statute of Limitations. The Statute of Limitations on rent which was the subject of an oral lease is usually two years from the time the rent was due. The Statute of Limitations on rent which was the subject of a written lease is usually four years. The time limit runs from the time the first monthly payment was due, so if a person, under an oral rental agreement owes for November, December, and January, you must file suit within two years from November.

Q. Must a lease be recorded with the county recorder?

A. No. But here is a good tenant tip. If you record the lease the landlord always has to come to you to get it "unrecorded" or it remains as a lien on his property. This could put him at your mercy. A lease must be acknowledged before a notary before it can be recorded.

Q. My landlord keeps coming into my apartment and looking around in my absence. How can I stop this?

A. Unless there is a provision in the lease which permits this, he is violating your right to quiet enjoyment. It could be grounds for breaking the lease.

Q. My tenant won't pay the rent and won't move. Can I shut off the water?

A. No. At least not in California. See Chapter 9.

Q. My landlord refuses to accept my check for rent. He insists on cash. It is inconvenient for me to pay in cash. Can he refuse my check?

A. Yes. A landlord is not required to accept a check.

Q. My landlord refuses to give me a receipt for my rent. Is he required to?

A. Yes. See Civil Code Section 1499.

Q. I paid a month's rent on November 1, gave written notice to move and moved on November 20th. Am I entitled to a refund?

A. No. See Chapter 4.

Q. Can a tenant waive his right to be served with a three-day notice to quit or pay rent in the event of a default?

A. No. The tenant's waiver would be void.

Q. Are the terms of a lease still in force if a tenant stays over after the expiration of the lease?

A. No. The tenant is, of course, still required to pay rent and it will be presumed that the rental will be the same as it was in the lease. The remaining provisions of the lease, however, will no longer be in force.

Q. The tenant is only able to pay half of his rent this month. Must I accept it?

A. No. A landlord is not required to accept anything less than the entire rent. You may accept it and still sue to evict him for nonpayment of rent.

Q. What if a landlord won't accept the entire amount of rent?

A. Sometimes a landlord won't accept rent so that he may evict a tenant for nonpayment without giving him 30 days' notice to quit. If the landlord won't accept your rent, deposit it in his bank account. See Civil Code Section 1500.

Q. Suppose the landlord and tenant desire to change some of the terms of the lease. How do they accomplish this?

A. The changes *must* be in writing. The changes may be written somewhere in the body of the original lease and initialed by both parties.

Q. Can the landlord and tenant agree to a reduction of the rent?

A. Usually, an agreement to reduce future rental payments will not be binding on a landlord. However, an acceptance in writing of a reduced amount for *past* rental payments will be binding on the landlord.

Q. Is an assignee or subtenant bound by the terms of the lease to which the original tenant agreed?

A. Yes. The landlord can enforce all of the provisions to which the original tenant agreed.

Q. I put a deposit on an apartment and later decided not to take the apartment. Why won't the landlord return my deposit?

A. Many prospective tenants ask this question and I don't know why they do. The purpose of a deposit is to provide the landlord with some assurance that you will rent the apartment. To deprive him of the deposit after you have broken your promise to rent the apartment would defeat the purpose of the deposit. See Chapter 1 for a detailed discussion on deposits.

Q. My rent was $150 per month. I paid $300 when I moved in and $150 each month thereafter. Now, the last month, the landlord wants another $150. Why?

A. When you moved in you probably paid a security deposit over the first month's rent. You thought it was first and last months' rent in advance. See the chapter os security deposits vs. prepaid rents.

Q. What is meant by the term "eminent domain" or "condemnation"?

A. "Eminent domain" is the power under which the government, whether federal, state or local, can take private property for public use. For example, if the state decides to construct a freeway and your home happens to be in the path of the proposed freeway, the state can condemn your property and a court, in a "condemnation" action, will award you compensation which must be paid by the state.

Q. I am behind in my rent. The landlord came in and took my stereo. Can he do this?

A. He can take none of your property without a court order. Even with a court order, your stereo may be exempt. See Chapter 8.

Q. My landlord has threatened me and harasses me at all hours of the night. This has caused me to be extremely nervous and upset. Is there anything I can do?

A. A tenant can recover for mental anguish caused by a landlord's behavior (or vice versa). This is true even if there was no physical injury. A recent California case resulted in an award to a tenant for emotional upset caused by a landlord's yelling and threats.

Q. I was late in the payment of my rent and my landlord locked me out. What can I do?

A. A landlord must comply with the unlawful detainer or abandonment statutes and cannot lock a tenant out for failure to pay rent. The tenant can sue if he is wrongfully locked out.

Q. Is my apartment rent deductible for income tax purposes?

A. Not for federal purposes unless a portion of the unit is used for bona fide business purposes. California provides a state income tax credit for apartment renters. The rate is based upon adjusted gross income.

Q. Can the landlord evict me because I organize a tenant's association?

A. One recent case says yes. Another indicates maybe not. That's not much help, but basically a landlord can evict a month to month tenant as he pleases, except for retaliatory eviction cases. See Chapter 11.

## APPENDIX

### *RECEIPT FOR DEPOSIT*

In consideration of $_____, the undersigned does hereby agree to hold Apt. No. _____ at _____ St., Los Angeles, Calif. to and including _____, 1972, for Tommy Tenant who agrees to accept said apartment on _____, 1972, at a rental of $ _____ per month payable in advance on the _____ day of _____, 1972, and on the _____ day of each month thereafter.

It is further agreed that if the prospective tenant does not take the apartment on said date, then the consideration herein mentioned shall be considered as and for the rental of said apartment from the date of this receipt to the said _____day of _____, 1972.

If the prospective tenant does take said apartment, then this deposit will be applied to the first month's rent.

_____

Larry Landlord

\* \* \* \* \*

### NOTICE RE CHANGE OF TERMS OF TENANCY

TO: TOMMY TENANT:

You are hereby notified that at the expiration of the thirty days after service on you of this notice, your month to month tenancy of the premises you now occupy will be changed as follows:

The rental will be at a rate of _____ Dollars per month instead of _____ Dollars per month. The rental will be payable monthly on the 1st day of each month.

LARRY LANDLORD

_____

# NOTICE TO PAY RENT OR QUIT

TO: TOMMY TENANT, Tenant in Possession.

WITHIN THREE DAYS, after the service on you of this notice, you are hereby required to pay the rent of the premises hereinafter described, of which you now hold possession, amounting to the sum of _____ Dollars ($____), being the monthly rent due from _____, 1972 to _____, 1972, or you are hereby required to deliver up possession of the hereinafter described premises, within three days after service on you of this notice, to the undersigned, Larry Landlord, owner, who is authorized to receive the same, or the undersigned will institute legal proceedings against you to declare the forfeiture of the lease or rental agreement under which you occupy the hereinbelow described property and to recover possession of said premises, with treble rents and damages.

The premises, herein referred to are situated in the City of _____, County of _____, State of California, designated by the number and street as _____, Apt. ___

You are further notified that the undersigned does hereby elect to declare the forfeiture of your lease or rental agreement under which you hold possession of the above described premises.

Dated this ___ day of _____, 1972.

_____
Larry Landlord, Owner

74

| NAME AND ADDRESS OF ATTORNEY: | TELEPHONE NO.: | For Court Use Only: |
|---|---|---|

ATTORNEY FOR:

Insert name of court, judicial district or branch court, if any, and Post Office and Street Address:

PLAINTIFF:

DEFENDANT:

| **SUMMONS   (UNLAWFUL DETAINER)** | Case Number: |
|---|---|

**NOTICE! You have been sued. The court may decide against you without your being heard unless you respond within 5 days. Read the information below.**

**¡AVISO! Usted ha sido demandado. El Tribunal puede decidir contra Ud. sin audiencia a menos que Ud. responda dentro de 5 días. Lea la información que sigue.**

1. TO THE DEFENDANT: A civil complaint has been filed by the plaintiff against you. (See footnote*)

   a. If you wish to defend this lawsuit, you must, within 5 days after this summons is served on you, file with this court a written pleading in response to the complaint. (If a Justice Court, you must file with the court a written pleading or cause an oral pleading to be entered in the docket in response to the complaint, within 5 days after this summons is served on you).

   b. Unless you so respond, your default will be entered upon application of the plaintiff and this court may enter a judgment against you for the relief demanded in the complaint, which could result in garnishment of wages, taking of money or property or other relief requested in the complaint.

   c. **If you wish to seek the advice of an attorney in this matter, you should do so promptly so that your pleading, if any, may be filed on time.**

Dated:. . . . . . . . . . . . . . . ., Clerk, By _____ , Deputy

(SEAL)

2. ☐ **NOTICE TO THE PERSON SERVED:** You are served
   a. ☐ As an individual defendant.
   b. ☐ As the person sued under the fictitious name of:  . . . . . . . . . .
   . . . . . . . . . . . . . . . . . . . . . . . . . . . . . . . . .
   c. ☐ On behalf of: . . . . . . . . . . . . . . . . . . . . . . . .
   . . . . . . . . . . . . . . . . . . . . . . . . . . . . . . . . .
   Under: ☐ CCP 416.10 (Corporation)          ☐ CCP 416.60 (Minor)
   ☐ CCP 416.20 (Defunct Corporation)          ☐ CCP 416.70 (Incompetent)
   ☐ CCP 416.40 (Association or Partnership)  ☐ CCP 416.90 (Individual)
   ☐ Other:

* The word "complaint" includes cross-complaint, "plaintiff" includes cross-complainant, "defendant" includes cross-defendant, singular includes the plural and masculine includes feminine and neuter. A written pleading, including an answer, demurrer, etc., must be in the form required by the California Rules of Court. Your original pleading must be filed in this court with proper filing fees and proof that a copy thereof was served on each plaintiff's attorney and on each plaintiff not represented by an attorney. The time when a summons is deemed served on a party may vary depending on the method of service. For example, see CCP 413.10 through 415.40.

Form Adopted by Rule 982 of
The Judicial Council of California
Revised Effective January 1, 1975

**(See reverse side for Proof of Service)**
**SUMMONS (UNLAWFUL DETAINER)**

CCP 412.20, 412.30, etc.
76S840—Ci 2—Cdb 12-74

MUNICIPAL COURT, PASADENA JUDICIAL DISTRICT

COUNTY OF LOS ANGELES, STATE OF CALIFORNIA

| | | |
|---|---|---|
| LARRY LANDLORD, | ) | |
| | ) | |
| Plaintiff, | ) | No. |
| | ) | |
| vs. | ) | COMPLAINT |
| | ) | (UNLAWFUL DETAINER) |
| TOMMY TENANT, | ) | |
| | ) | |
| Defendant. | ) | |

Plaintiff complains:

1.  The defendant at all times herein mentioned did and now does reside in the Pasadena Judicial District, County of Los Angeles, State of California.

2.  That within two years last past the plaintiff leased to the defendant the premises located at and described as 19 Elm Street, Pasadena, Apartment #3, for a monthly rental of $70.00 per month, payable in advance on the 24th day of each month.  Said tenancy was on a month-to-month basis.

3.  The plaintiff is the owner and entitled to possession of the above-described premises.

4.  Within two years last past defendant went into possession of said premises under said month-to-month tenancy and has been and now is in actual possession thereof.

5.  That under the terms of said lease $70.00 became due and payable on September 24, 1971 as rent for the month of

September 24, 1971 to October 23, 1971. This sum has not been
paid by defendant and is due, owing and unpaid.

6. Demand has been made upon defendant to pay said
sum, but defendant has wholly failed, refused and neglected to
pay that sum or any part thereof.

7. That on October 27, 1971 plaintiff served or caused
to be served on defendant a notice in writing stating the amount
of rent due and required payment thereof or possession of said
premises within three days after the service of said notice, upon
condition that if said rent was not paid within said time, plaintiff was to institute legal proceedings against defendant to
recover possession of said premises. Plaintiff by this action
does elect to declare a forfeiture of the tenancy.

8. More than three days have elapsed since the service
of said notice on defendant, but no part of said rent, to wit,
the sum of $70.00, has been paid and said sum still remains due,
owing and unpaid.

9. That defendant refused and does now refuse to surrender possession of said premises and continues in possession
thereof without the consent or permission of the plaintiff.

WHEREFORE, plaintiff prays:

1. For judgment in the sum of $70.00 rent;

2. For restitution of said premises and forfeiture of
the tenancy;

3. For such other and further sums as may accrue as
rent of said premises pursuant to said lease and prior to rendi-
tion of judgment herein;

4. For treble damages; and

5. For costs of suit and such other relief as the
Court deems just.

                                    LARRY  LANDLORD
                                    ---------------------
                                    LARRY  LANDLORD

77

# RENTAL AGREEMENT

## (MONTH - TO - MONTH TENANCY)

THIS AGREEMENT, entered into this_____day of_____, 19_____, by and between

_____ and _____, hereinafter called
respectively lessor and lessee.

WITNESSETH: That for and in consideration of the payment of the rents and the performance of the covenants contained on the part of lessee, said lessor does hereby demise and let unto the lessee, and lessee hires from lessor for use as a residence those certain premises described as

_____ located at

_____ Street, _____, California, for a

tenancy from month-to-month commencing on the _____ day of _____, 19_____, and at a

monthly rental of _____ ($_____) Dollars per month,

payable monthly in advance on the_____day of each and every month.

It is further mutually agreed between the parties as follows:

(1) Said premises shall be occupied by no more than_____adults and _____ children.

(2) Lessee shall not keep or permit to be kept in said premises any dog, cat, parrot, or other bird or animal.

(3) Lessee shall not violate any city ordinance or state law in or about said premises.

(4) That all alterations, additions, or improvements made in and to said premises shall, unless otherwise provided by written agreement between the parties hereto, be the property of Lessor and shall remain upon and be surrendered with the premises.

(5) Lessee shall not sub-let the demised premises, or any part thereof, or assign this agreement without the lessor's written consent.

(6) Any failure by lessee to pay rent or other charges promptly when due, or to comply with any other term or condition hereof, shall at the option of the lessor forthwith terminate this tenancy.

(7) Lessee shall keep and maintain the premises in a clean and sanitary condition at all times, and upon the termination of the tenancy shall surrender the premises to the lessor in as good condition as when received, ordinary wear and damage by the elements excepted.

(8) Lessee hereby waives all right to make repairs at the expense of lessor as provided in Section 1942 of the Civil Code of the State of California, and all rights provided in Section 1941 of said Civil Code.

(9) The _____ agrees to properly cultivate, care for, and adequately water the lawn, shrubbery, trees and grounds.

(10) The _____ shall pay for all water supplied to the said premises. The lessee shall pay for all gas, heat, light, power, telephone service, and all other services, except as herein provided, supplied to the said premises.

(11) Nothing contained in this agreement shall be construed as waiving any of lessor's rights under the laws of the State of California.

(12) This agreement and the tenancy hereby granted may be terminated at any time by either party hereto by giving to the other party not less than

_____ (_____) days prior notice in writing.

(13) If an action be brought for the recovery of rent or other moneys due or to become due under this lease or by reason of a breach of any covenant herein contained or for the recovery of the possession of said premises, or to compel the performance of anything agreed to be done by Lessee, or to recover for damages to said property, or to enjoin any act contrary to the provisions hereof, Lessee will pay to Lessor all of the costs in connection therewith, including, but not by way of limitation, reasonable attorney's fees, whether or not the action proceed to judgment.

(14) Remarks:


IN WITNESS WHEREOF the parties hereto have executed this agreement in duplicate the day and year first above written.


_____          _____
                Lessor                                      Lessee

78

## EXCERPTS FROM THE CALIFORNIA
## CODE OF CIVIL PROCEDURE (CCP)
### Note: These excerpts have been abbreviated.

CCP SEC. 116.2  JURISDICTION

The small claims division shall have jurisdiction in action:

(a) For recovery of money only where the amount of the demand does not exceed seven hundred fifty dollars ($750);

(b) To enforce payment of delinquent unsecured personal property taxes in an amount not to exceed seven hundred fifty dollars ($750), if the legality of the tax is not contested by the defendant;

(c) In unlawful detainer, after default in rent for residential property, where the term of tenancy is not greater than month to month and the amount claimed does not exceed seven hundred fifty dollars ($750).

CCP SEC. 116.4  COMMENCEMENT OF ACTION

(a) An action shall be commenced by the plaintiff's filing, in person or by mail with the judge or clerk of the small claims division, a claim under oath setting forth: the name and address of the defendant; the amount and the basis of the claim; and that the plaintiff has demanded payment and, in applicable cases, the possession of the property; that the defendant has failed or refused to pay, and where applicable, has refused to surrender the premises; and that the plaintiff understands that the judgment on his claim will be conclusive without right of appeal by him.

(b) The judge or clerk shall thereupon do either of the following:

(1) The judge or clerk shall (i) sign an order directing a defendant who resides within the county in which the action is filed, to appear on a hearing date not more than 40 days nor less than 10 days from the

date of the order or, if the defendant resides outside of the county in which the action is filed, to appear on a hearing date not more than 70 days nor less than 30 days from the date of the order, (ii) cause a copy of the claim and order to be mailed to the defendant by any form of mail providing for a return receipt, or cause a copy to be delivered to defendant in person, and (iii) inform the plaintiff of a specified hearing date and direct him to appear on that date with witnesses and documents to prove his claim.

(2) The judge or clerk shall (i) cause a copy of any claim to be mailed to the defendant by any form of mail providing for a return receipt or cause a copy to be delivered to defendant in person, (ii) upon proof of service in accordance with subparagraph (i), sign an order setting a hearing date for a defendant who resides within the county in which the action is filed of not more than 40 days nor less than 10 days from the date of receipt of proof of service or, if the defendant resides outside of the county in which the action is filed, a hearing date of not more than 70 days nor less than 30 days from the date of receipt of service, (iii) cause a copy of the order setting the hearing date and directing the defendant to appear on such date to be served upon the defendant as provided in subparagraph (i), and (iv) cause a copy of the order setting the hearing date and directing the plaintiff to appear on such date with witness and documents to prove his claim to be served upon the plaintiff as provided in subparagraph (i).

Service by such methods shall be deemed complete on the date of personal service, or on the date that the defendant signs the mail return receipt, or upon the presentation of other competent evidence to the court, whichever is applicable. Service of a copy of the claim and order may also be made and shall be complete, as provided in subdivision (a) or (b) of Section 415.20 of this code, without requirement for attempted service by either of the methods above provided, and shall be complete as provided in Section 415.20. Service to be valid must be made within this state. If in the case of paragraph (1) of this subdivision, the service of the claim and order upon the defendant is not completed at least five days prior to the hearing date where the defendant resides within the county in which the action is brought, or at least 15 days prior to the hearing date where the defendant resides outside the county in which the action is brought, or at least 15 days prior to the hearing date where the defendant resides outside the county in which the action is brought, unless the defendant personally appears and does not request a continuance, the court shall continue the date for the hearing for at least 10 days, and shall cause notice thereof by first-class mail to be served on any defendant who has been served but did not personally appear.

CCP SEC. 116.8  PLEADING: DEFENDANT'S CLAIM

(a) No formal pleading other than the claim and order are necessary. The defendant may file a claim in the same proceeding in an amount not to exceed seven hundred fifty dollars ($750). In the event the defendant files such a claim in the court, he shall serve a copy of his claim on the plaintiff at least five days before the hearing date, unless the plaintiff has served him 10 days or less before the hearing date in which case he shall serve a copy of his claim at least one day before the hearing date. Defendant shall file and serve his claim in the manner provided for filing and serving a claim under Section 116.4

(b) If defendant has a claim against plaintiff in an amount over the jurisdiction of the small claims court as set forth in Section 116.2, but of a nature which would be the subject of a cross-complaint under the rules of pleading and practice governing the superior court, then defendant may commence an action against plaintiff in a court of competent jurisdiction and file with the small claims court wherein plaintiff has commenced his action, at or before the time set for the trial of said small claims actions, an affidavit setting forth the facts of the commencement of such action by such defendant. He shall attach to such affidavit a true copy of the complaint so filed by defendant against plaintiff, and pay to the clerk of the small claims court the sum of one dollar ($1) for a transmittal fee, and shall deliver to plaintiff in person a copy of the affidavit and complaint at or before the time above stated. Thereupon the small claims court action shall be transferred to the court set forth in the affidavit, and shall transmit all files and papers in the small claims actions to such other court, and the actions shall then be tried together in such other court.

The plaintiff in the small claims action shall not be required to pay to the clerk of the court to which the action is so transferred any transmittal, appearance, or filing fee in said action, but shall be required to pay the filing and any other fee required of a defendant if he appears in the action filed against him.

## CCP SEC.732. WASTE; PARTIES TO ACTION; RIGHT OF ACTION; TREBLE DAMAGES

WASTE, ACTIONS FOR. If a guardian, tenant for life or years, joint tenant, or tenant in common of real property, commit waste thereon, any person aggrieved by the waste may bring an action against him therefor, in which action there may be judgment for treble damages.

## CCP SEC.1159. FORCIBLE ENTRY DEFINED

Every person is guilty of a forcible entry who either:

1. By breaking open doors, windows, or other parts of a house, or by any kind of violence or circumstance of terror enters upon or into any real property; or,

2. Who, after entering peaceably upon real property, turns out by force, threats, or menacing conduct, the party in possession.

## CCP SEC.1160. FORCIBLE DETAINER DEFINED

Every person is guilty of a forcible detainer who either:

1. By force, or by menaces and threats of violence, unlawfully holds and keeps the possession of any real property, whether the same was acquired peaceably or otherwise; or,

2. Who, in the night-time, or during the absence of the occupant of any lands, unlawfully enters upon real property, and who, after demand

made for the surrender thereof, for the period of five days, refuses to surrender the same to such former occupant.

The occupant of real property, within the meaning of this subdivision, is one who, within five days preceding such unlawful entry, was in the peaceable and undisturbed possession of such lands.

## CCP SEC. 1161 UNLAWFUL DETAINER DEFINED

A tenant of real property, for a term less than life, or the executor or administrator of his estate heretofore qualified and now acting or hereafter to be qualified and act, is guilty of unlawful detainer:

1. When he continues in possession, in person or by subtenant, of the property, or any part thereof, after the expiration of the term for which it is let to him; provided such expiration is of a nondefault nature however brought about without the permission of his landlord, or the successor in estate of his landlord, if any there be; including the case where the person to be removed became the occupant of the premises as a servant, employee, agent, or licensee and the relation of master and servant or employer and employee or principal and agent or licensor and licensee has been lawfully terminated or the time fixed for such occupancy by the agreement between the parties has expired; but nothing in this subdivision contained shall be construed as preventing the removal of such occupant in any other lawful manner; but in case of a tenancy at will, it must first be terminated by notice, as perscribed in the Civil Code.

3. When he continues in possession, in person or by subtenant, after a neglect or failure to perform other conditions or covenants of the lease or agreement under which the property is held, including any covenant not to assign or sublet, than the one for the payment of rent, and three days' notice, in writing, requiring the performance of such conditions or covenants, or the possession of the property, shall have been served upon him, and if there is a subtenant in actual occupation of the premises, also, upon such subtenant. Within three days after the service of the notice, the tenant, or any subtenant in actual occupation of the premises, or any mortgagee of the term, or other person interested in its continuance, may perform the conditions or covenants of the lease or pay the stipulated rent, as the case may be, and thereby save the lease from forfeiture; provided, if the conditions and covenants of the lease, violated by the lessee, cannot afterward be performed, then no notice, as last perscribed herein, need be given to said lessee or his subtenant, demanding the performance of the violated conditions or covenants of the lease.

A tenant may take proceedings, similar to those perscribed in this chapter, to obtain possession of the premises let to a subtenant or held by a servant, employee, agent, or licensee, in case of his unlawful detention of the premises underlet to him or held by him.

2. When he continues in possession, in person or by subtenant, without the permission of his landlord, or the successor in estate of his landlord, if any there be, after default in the payment of rent, pursuant to the lease or agreement under which the property is held, and three days' notice, in writing, requiring its payment, stating the amount which is due, or possession of the property, shall have been served upon him and if there is a subtenant in actual occupation of the premises, also upon such subtenant.

Such notice may be served at any time within one year after the rent becomes due. In all cases of tenancy upon agricultural lands, where the tenant has held over and retained possession for more than 60 days, after the expiration of the term without any demand of possession or notice to quit by the landlord or the successor in estate of his landlord, if any there be, he shall be deemed to be holding by permission of the landlord or successor in estate of his landlord, if any there be, and shall be entitled to hold under the terms of the lease for another full year, and shall not be guilty of an unlawful detainer during said year, and such holding over for the period aforesaid shall be taken and construed as a consent on the part of a tenant to hold for another year.

## CCP SEC.1162.  NOTICE; METHODS OF SERVICE

The notices required by sections 1161 and 1161a may be served, either:

1.   By delivering a copy to the tenant personally; or,

2.   If he be absent from his place of residence, and from his usual place of business, by leaving a copy with some person of suitable age and discretion at either place, and sending a copy through the mail addressed to the tenant at his place of residence; or,

3.   If such place of residence and business cannot be ascertained, or a person of suitable age or discretion there can not be found, then by affixing a copy in a conspicuous place on the property, and also delivering a copy to a person there residing, if such person can be found; and also sending a copy through the mail addressed to the tenant at the place where the property is situated. Service upon a subtenant may be made in the same manner.


## CCP SEC.1166a.  WRIT OF POSSESSION; ISSUANCE AND DIRECTION; GROUNDS; UNDERTAKING; LIMITATION ON DEFENDANT'S DAMAGE ACTION

Upon filing the complaint, the plaintiff may, upon motion have immediate possession of the premises by a writ of possession issued by the court and directed to the sheriff of the county, or constable or marshal, for execution, where it appears to the satisfaction of the court, after a hearing on the motion, from the verified complaint and from any affidavits filed or oral testimony given by or on behalf of the parties, that the defendant resides out of state, has departed from the state, cannot, after due diligence, be found within the state, or has concealed himself to avoid the service of summons. Written notice of the hearing on the motion shall be served on the defendant by the plaintiff in accordance with the provisions of Section 1011, and shall inform the defendant that he may file affidavits on his behalf with the court and may appear and present testimony on his behalf, and that, if he fails to appear, the plaintiff will apply to the court for the writ of possession. The plaintiff shall file an undertaking with good and sufficient sureties, to be approved by the judge, in such sum as shall be fixed and determined by the judge, to the effect that, if the plaintiff fails to recover judgment against the defendant for the possession of the premises or if the suit is dismissed, the plaintiff will pay to the defendant such damages, not to exceed the amount fixed in the undertaking, as may be sustained by the defendant by reason of such dispossession under the writ of possession. An action to recover such damages shall be commenced by the defendant in a court of competent jurisdiction within one year from the date of entry of dismissal or of final judgment in favor of the defendant.

CCP SEC. 1174.   JUDGMENT: DAMAGES: STAY OF EXECUTION: ENFORCEMENT OF JUDGMENT.

(a) If upon the trial, the verdict of the jury, or, if the case be tried without a jury, the findings of the court be in favor of the plaintiff and against the defendant, judgment shall be entered for the restitution of the premises; and if the proceedings be for an unlawful detainer after neglect, or failure to perform the conditions or covenants of the lease or agreement under which the property is held, or after default in the payment of rent, the judgment shall also declare the forfeiture of such lease or agreement if the notice required by Section 1161 of the code states the election of the landlord to declare the forfeiture thereof, but if such notice does not so state such election, the lease or agreement shall not be forfeited.

(b) The jury or the court, if the proceedings be tried without a jury, shall also assess the damages occasioned to the plaintiff by any forcible entry, or by any forcible or unlawful detainer, alleged in the complaint and proved on the trial, and find the amount of any rent due, if the alleged unlawful detainer be after default in the payment of rent. If the defendant is found guilty of forcible entry, or forcible or unlawful detainer, and malice is shown, the plaintiff may be awarded either damages and rent found due or punitive damages in an amount which does not exceed three times the amount of damages and rent found due. The trier of fact shall determine whether damages and rent found due or punitive damages shall be awarded, and judgment shall be entered accordingly.

(c) When the proceeding is for an unlawful detainer after default in the payment of rent, and the lease or agreement under which the rent is payable has not by its terms expired, and the notice required by Section 1161 has not stated the election of the landlord to declare the forfeiture thereof, the court may, and, if the lease or agreement is in writing, is for a term of more than one year, and does not contain a forfeiture clause, shall order that execution upon the judgment shall not be issued until the expiration of five days after the entry of the judgment, within which time the tenant, or any subtenant, or any mortgagee of the term, or any other party interested in its continuance, may pay into the court, for the landlord, the amount found due as rent, with interest thereon, and the amount of the damages found by the jury or the court for the unlawful detainer, and the costs of the proceedings, and thereupon the judgment shall be satisfied and the tenant be restored to his estate.

But if payment as here provided be not made within five days, the judgment may be enforced for its full amount, and for the possession of the premises. In all other cases the judgment may be enforced immediately.

(d) A plaintiff, having obtained a writ of restitution of the premises pursuant to an action for unlawful detainer, shall be entitled to have the premises restored to him by officers charged with the enforcement of such writs. Promptly upon payment of reasonable costs of service, the enforcing officer shall serve an occupant or post a copy of the writ in the same manner as upon levy of writ of attachment pursuant to subdivision (d) of Section 488.310. In addition, where the copy is posted on the property, another copy of the writ shall thereafter be mailed to the defendant at his business or residence address last known to the plaintiff or his attorney or, if no such address is known, at the premises. The writ of restitution of the premises shall include a statement that personal property remaining on the premises at the time of its restitution to the landlord will be sold or otherwise disposed of in accordance with Section 1174 of the Code of Civil Procedure unless the tenant or the owner pays the landlord the reasonable cost of storage and takes possession of the personal property not later than 15 days after the time the premises are restored to the landlord. If the tenant does not vacate the premises within five days from the date of service, or, if the copy of the writ is posted, within five days from the date of mailing of the additional notice, the enforcing officer shall remove the tenant from the premises and place the plaintiff in possession thereof.

# EXCERPTS FROM THE
# CALIFORNIA CIVIL CODE
# (CC)

Note: These sections have been abbreviated.

## CC SEC.660.  FIXTURES DEFINED

A thing is deemed to be affixed to land when it is attached to it by roots, as in the case of trees, vines, or shrubs; or imbedded in it, as in the case of walls; or permanently resting upon it, as in the case of buildings; or permanently attached to what is thus permanent, as by means of cement, plaster, nails, bolts, or screws; except that for the purposes of sale, emblements, industrial growing crops and things attached to or forming part of the land, which are agreed to be severed before sale or under the contract of sale, shall be treated as goods and be governed by the provisions of the title of this code regulating the sales of goods.

## CC SEC.789.3.  INTERRUPTION OF UTILITIES SERVICE

(a)  A landlord shall not with intent to terminate the occupancy under any lease or other tenancy or estate at will, however created, of property used by a tenant as his residence willfully cause, directly or indirectly, the interruption or termination of any utility service furnished the tenant, including but not limited to, water, heat, light, electricity, gas, telephone, elevator, or refrigeration, whether or not the utility service is under the control of the landlord.

(b)  Any landlord who violates this section shall be liable to the tenant in a civil action for all of the following:

(1)  Actual damages of the tenant.

(2)  One hundred dollars ($100) for each day or part thereof the tenant is deprived of utility service.

(c)  In any action under subdivision (b), the court shall award reasonable attorney's fees to the prevailing party.

## CC SEC.1019.  TENANTS: REMOVAL OF FIXTURES

A tenant may remove from the demised premises, any time during the continuance of his term, anything affixed thereto for purposes of trade, manufacture, ornament, or domestic use, if the removal can be effected without injury to the premises, unless the thing has, by the manner in which it is affixed, become an integral part of the premises.

## CC SEC.1499.  RECEIPT FOR PROPERTY DELIVERED IN PERFORMANCE

A debtor has a right to require from his creditor a written receipt for any property delivered in performance of his obligation.

## CC SEC.1500.  OFFER OF PAYMENT; DEPOSIT; NOTICE

An obligation for the payment of money is extinguished by a due offer of payment, if the amount is immediately deposited in the name of the creditor, with some bank of deposit within this State, of good repute, and notice thereof is given to the creditor.

## CC SEC.1861a.  KEEPERS OF APARTMENT HOUSES, ETC; LIEN; ENFORCEMENT PROCEDURE; DISPOSITION OF PROCEEDS; EXEMPTIONS

Keepers of furnished and unfurnished apartment houses, apartments, cottages, or bungalow courts shall have a lien upon the baggage and other property of value belonging to their tenants or guests, and upon all the right, title and interest of their tenants or guests in and to all property in the possession of such tenants or guests which may be in such apartment house, apartment, cottage, or bungalow court, for the proper charges due from such tenants or guests, for their accommodation, rent, services, meals, and such extras as are furnished at their request, and for all moneys expended for them, at their request, and for the costs of enforcing such lien.

Such lien may be enforced only after final judgment in an action brought to recover such charges or moneys. During the pendency of the proceeding, the plaintiff may take possession of such baggage and property upon an order issued by the court, where it appears to the satisfaction of the court from an affidavit filed by or on behalf of the plaintiff that the baggage or property is about to be destroyed, substantially devalued, or removed from the premises. Ten days written notice of the hearing on the motion for such order shall be served on the defendant and shall inform the defendant that he may file affidavits on his behalf and present testimony in his behalf and that if he fails to appear the plaintiff will apply to the court for such order. The plaintiff shall file an undertaking with good and sufficient sureties, to be approved by the court, in such sum as may be fixed by the court.

Upon such order, the plaintiff shall have the right to enter peaceably the unfurnished apartment house, apartment, cottage, or bungalow court used by his guest or tenant without liability to such guest or tenant, including any possible claim of liability for conversion, trespass, or forcible entry. The plaintiff shall have the same duties and liabilities as a depository for hire as to property which he takes into his possession. An entry shall be considered peaceable when accomplished with a key or passkey or through an unlocked door during the hours between sunrise and sunset. Unless the judgment shall be paid within 30 days from the date when it becomes final, the plaintiff may sell the baggage and property, at public auction to the highest bidder, after giving notice of such sale by publication of a notice containing the name of the debtor, the amount due, a brief description of the property to be sold, and the time and place of such sale, pursuant to Section 6064 of the Government Code in the county in which said apartment house, apartment, cottage, or bungalow court is situated, and after by mailing, at least 15 days prior to the date of sale, a copy of such notice addressed to such tenant or guest at his residence or other known address, and if not known, such notice shall be addressed to such tenant or guest at the place where such apartment house, apartment, cottage, or bungalow court is situated; and, after satisfying such lien out of the proceeds of such sale, together with any reasonable costs, that may have been incurred in enforcing said lien, the residue of said proceeds of sale, if any, shall, upon demand made within six months after such sale, be paid to such tenant or guest; and if not demanded within six months from the date of such sale, said residue, if any, shall be paid into the treasury of the county in which such sale took place; and if the same be not claimed by the owner thereof, or his legal representative within one year thereafter, it shall be paid into the general fund of the county; and such sale shall be a perpetual bar to any action against said keeper for the recovery of such baggage or property, or of the value thereof, or for any damages, growing out of the failure of such tenant or guest to receive such baggage or property.

When the baggage and property are not in the possession of the keeper as provided herein, such lien shall be enforced only by writ of execution.

This section does not apply to:

(a) Any musical instrument of any kind or description which is used by the owner thereof to earn all or a part of his living.

(b) Any prosthetic or orthopedic appliance, or any medicine, drug, or medical equipment or health apparatus, personally used by a tenant or guest, or a member of his family who is residing with him.

(c) Table and kitchen furniture, including one refrigerator, washing machine, sewing machine, stove; bedroom furniture, one overstuffed chair, one davenport, one dining table and chairs, and also all tools, instruments, clothing and books used by the tenant or guest in gaining a livelihood; beds, bedding and bedsteads, oil paintings and drawings drawn or painted by any member of the family of the tenant or guest, and any family portraits and their necessary frames.

(d) All other household, table or kitchen furniture not expressly mentioned in paragraph (c), including but not limited to radios, television sets, phonographs, records, motor vehicles that may be stored on the premises except so much of any such articles as may be reasonably sufficient to satisfy the lien provided for by this section; and provided further, that such lien shall be secondary to the claim of any prior bona fide holder of a chattel mortgage on and the rights of a conditional seller of such articles, other than the tenant or guest. Any property which is exempt from attachment or execution under the provisions of the Code of Civil Procedure shall not be subject to the lien provided for in this section.

## CC SEC.1928. DEGREE OF CARE

The hirer of a thing must use ordinary care for its preservation in safety and in good condition.

## CC SEC.1929. REPAIRS

The hirer of a thing must repair all deteriorations or injuries thereto occasioned by his want of ordinary care.

## CC SEC.1941. BUILDING FOR HUMAN OCCUPANCY; FITNESS; REPAIRS

The lessor of a building intended for the occupation of human beings must, in the absence of an agreement to the contrary, put it into a condition fit for such occupation, and repair all subsequent dilapidations thereof, which render it untenantable, except such as are mentioned in section nineteen hundred and twenty-nine.

## CC SEC.1941.1 UNTENANTABLE DWELLINGS

A dwelling shall be deemed untenantable for purposes of Section 1941 if it substantially lacks any of the following affirmative standard characteristics:

(a) Effective waterproofing and weather protection of roof and exterior walls, including unbroken windows and doors.

(b)   Plumbing facilities which conformed to applicable law in effect at the time of installation, maintained in good working order.

(c)   A water supply approved under applicable law, which is under the control of the tenant, capable of producing hot and cold running water, or a system which is under the control of the landlord, which produces hot and cold running water, furnished to appropriate fixtures, and connected to a sewage disposal system approved under applicable law.

(d)   Heating facilities which conformed with applicable law at the time of installation, maintained in good working order.

(e)   Electrical lighting, with wiring and electrical equipment which conformed with applicable law at the time of installation, maintained in good working order.

(f)   Building, grounds and appurtenances at the time of the commencement of the lease or rental agreement in every part clean, sanitary, and free from all accumulations of debris, filth, rubbish, garbage, rodents and vermin, and all areas under control of the landlord kept in every part clean, sanitary, and free from all accumulations of debris, filth, rubbish, garbage, rodents, and vermin.

(g)   An adequate number of appropriate receptacles for garbage and rubbish, in clean condition and good repair at the time of commencement of the lease or rental agreement, with the landlord providing appropriate serviceable receptacles thereafter, and being responsible for the clean condition and good repair of such receptacles under his control.

(h)   Floors, stairways, and railing maintained in good repair.

## CC SEC.1941.2   LESSEE'S AFFIRMATIVE OBLIGATIONS

(a)   No duty on the part of the lessor shall arise under Section 1941 or 1942 if the lessee is in substantial violation of any of the following affirmative obligations:

(1)   To keep that part of the premises which he occupies and uses clean and sanitary as the condition of the premises permits.

(2)   To dispose from his dwelling unit of all rubbish, garbage and other waste, in a clean and sanitary manner.

(3)   To properly use and operate all electrical, gas and plumbing fixtures and keep them as clean and sanitary as their condition permits.

92

(4)   Not to permit any person on the premises, with his permission, to willfully or wantonly destroy, deface, damage, impair or remove any part of the structure or dwelling unit or the facilities, equipment, or appurtenances thereto, nor himself do any such thing.

(5)   To occupy the premises as his abode, utilizing portions thereof for living, sleeping, cooking or dining purposes only which were respectively designed or intended to be used for such occupancies.

(b)   Paragraphs (1) and (2) of subdivision (a) shall not apply if the lessor has expressly agreed in writing to perform the act or acts mentioned therein.

## CC SEC. 1942.   REPAIRS BY LESSEE; RENT DEDUCTION; LIMIT

(a)   If within a reasonable time after notice to the lessor, of dilapidations which he ought to repair, he neglects to do so, the lessee may repair the same himself, where the cost of such repairs does not require an expenditure greater than one month's rent of the premises, and deduct the expenses of such repairs from the rent, or the lessee may vacate the premises, in which case he shall be discharged from further payment of rent, or performance of other conditions. This remedy shall not be available to the lessee more than once in any 12-month period.

(b)   For the purposes of this section, if a lessee acts to repair and deduct after the 30th day following notice, he is presumed to have acted after a reasonable time. The presumption established by this subdivision is a presumption affecting the burden of producing evidence.

## CC   SEC.1942.1   WAIVER OF RIGHTS; PUBLIC POLICY; ARBITRATION OF UNTENANTABILITY

Any agreement by a lessee of a dwelling waiving or modifying his rights under Section 1941 or 1942 shall be void as contrary to public policy with respect to any condition which renders the premises untenantable, except that the lessor and the lessee may agree that the lessee shall undertake to improve, repair or maintain all of stipulated portions of the dwelling as part of the consideration for rental.

The lessor and lessee may, if an agreement is in writing, set forth the provisions of Sections 1941 to 1942.1, inclusive, and provide that any controversy relating to a condition of the premises claimed to make them untenantable may by application of either party be submitted to arbitration, pursuant to the provisions of Title 9 (commencing with Section 1280), Part 3 of the Code of Civil Procedure, and that the costs of such arbitration shall be apportioned by the arbitrator between the parties.

## CC SEC.1942.5   RETALIATION; PROHIBITED ACTS

(a)   If the lessor has as his dominant purpose retaliation against the lessee because of the exercise by the lessee of his rights under this chapter or because of his complaint to an appropriate governmental agency as to tentability of a dwelling, and if the lessee of a dwelling is not in default as to the payment of his rent, the lessor may not recover possession of a dwelling in any action or proceeding, cause the lessee to quit involuntarily, increase the rent, or decrease any services, within 60 days:

(1)   After the date upon which the lessee, in good faith, has given notice pursuant to Section 1942; or

(2)   After the date upon which the lessee, in good faith, has filed a written complaint, with an appropriate governmental agency, of which the lessor has notice, for the purpose of obtaining correction of a condition relating to tenantability; or

(3)   After the date of an inspection or issuance of a citation, resulting from a written complaint described in paragraph (2) of which the lessor did not have notice; or

(4)   After entry of judgment or the signing of an arbitration award, if any, when in the judicial proceeding or arbitration the issue of tenantability is determined adversely to the lessor.

In each instance, the 60-day period shall run from the latest applicable date referred to in paragraphs (1) to (4), inclusive.

(b)   A lessee may not invoke the provisions of this section more than once in any 12-month period.

(c)   Nothing in this section shall be construed as limiting in any way the exercise by the lessor of his rights under any lease or agreement or any law pertaining to the hiring of property or his right to do any of the acts described in subdivision (a) for any lawful cause. Any waiver by a lessee of his rights under this section shall be void as contrary to public policy.

(d)   Notwithstanding the provisions of subdivisions (a) to (c), inclusive, a lessor may recover possession of a dwelling and do any of the other acts described in subdivision (a) within the period or periods prescribed therein if the notice of termination, rent increase, or other act, and any pleading or statement of issues in an arbitration, if any, states the ground upon which the lessor, in good faith, seeks to recover possession, increase rent, or do any of the other acts described in subdivision (a). If such statement be controverted, the lessor shall establish its truth at the trial or other hearing.

## CC SEC.1945. RENEWAL BY CONTINUED POSSESSION AND ACCEPTANCE OF RENT

If a lessee of real property remains in possession thereof after the expiration of the hiring, and the lessor accepts rent from him, the parties are presumed to have renewed the hiring on the same terms and for the same time, not exceeding one month when the rent is payable monthly, nor in any case one year.

## CC SEC.1945.5 AUTOMATIC RENEWAL OR EXTENSION; RECITALS IN CONTRACT; SIZE OF TYPE, ETC.

Notwithstanding any other provision of law, any term of a lease executed after the effective date of this section for the hiring of residential real property which provides for the automatic renewal or extension of the lease for all or part of the full term of the lease if the lessee remains in possession after the expiration of the lease or fails to give notice of his intent not to renew or extend before the expiration of the lease shall be null and void unless such renewal or extension provision appears in at least eight-point boldface type, if the contract is printed, in the body of the lease agreement and a recital of the fact that such provision is contained in body of the agreement appears in at least eight-point boldface type, if the contract is printed, immediately prior to the place where the lessee executes the agreement. In such case, the presumption in Section 1945 of this code shall apply.

Any waiver of the provisions of this section is void.

## CC SEC.1946. RENEWABLE HIRING; NOTICE OF TERMINATION

A hiring of real property, for a term not specified by the parties, is deemed to be renewed as stated in the last section, at the end of the term implied by law unless one of the parties gives written notice to the other of his intention to terminate the same, at least as long before the expiration thereof as the term of the hiring itself, not exceeding 30 days; provided, however, that as to tenancies from month to month either of the parties may terminate the same by giving at least 30 days' written notice thereof at any time and the rent shall be due and payable to and including the date of termination. It shall be competent for the parties to provide by an agreement at the time such tenancy is created that a notice of the intention to terminate the same may be given at any time not less than seven days before the expiration of the term thereof. The notice herein required shall be given in the manner prescribed in Section 1162 of the Code of Civil Procedure.

## CC SEC.1947.  RENT; TIME OF PAYMENT

When there is no usage or contract to the contrary, rents are payable at the termination of the holding, when it does not exceed one year. If the holding is by the day, week, month, quarter, or year, rent is payable at the termination of the respective periods, as it successively becomes due.

## CCP SEC. 1950.5  SECURITY FOR PERFORMANCE OF RENTAL AGREEMENT FOR RESIDENTIAL PROPERTY

As used in this section, "security" means any payment, fee, deposit or charge, including, but not limited to, an advance payment of rent, used or to be used for any purpose, including, but not limited to, any of the following:

(1) The compensation of a landlord for a tenant's default in the payment of rent.

(2) The repair of damages to the premises caused by the tenant.

(3) The cleaning of the premises upon termination of the tenancy.

A landlord may not demand or receive security, however denominated, in an amount or value in excess of an amount equal to two months' rent, in the case of unfurnished residential property, and an amount equal to three months' rent in the case of furnished residential property, in addition to any rent for the first month paid on or before initial occupancy. This subdivision shall not be construed to prohibit an advance payment of not less than six months' rent where the term of the lease is six months or longer.

This subdivision shall not be construed to preclude a landlord and a tenant from entering into a mutual agreement for the landlord, at the request of the tenant and for a specified fee or charge, to make structural, decorative furnishing, or other similar alterations, such alterations being other than that cleaning or repairing for which the landlord may charge the previous tenant as provided by subdivision (e).

The landlord may claim of the security only such amounts as are reasonably necessary to remedy tenant defaults in the payment of rent, to repair damages to the premises caused by the tenant, exclusive of ordinary wear and tear, or to clean such premises, if necessary, upon termination of the tenancy. No later than two weeks after the tenant has vacated the premises, the landlord shall furnish the tenant with an itemized written statement of the basis for, and the amount of, any security received and the disposition of such security and shall return any remaining portion of such security to the tenant.

The bad faith claim or retention by a landlord or transferee of a security or any portion thereof, in violation of this section, may subject the landlord or his transferee to damages not to exceed two hundred dollars ($200), in addition to any actual damages. In any action under this section, the landlord shall have the burden of proof as to the reasonableness of the amounts claimed.

No lease or rental agreement shall contain any provision characterizing any security as "nonrefundable."


## CC SEC.1951.2. TERMINATION OF LEASE; REMEDY OF LESSOR

(a) Except as otherwise provided in Section 1951.4, if a lessee of real property breaches the lease and abandons the property before the end of the term or if his right to possession is terminated by the lessor because of a breach of the lease, the right to possession is terminated by the lessor because of a breach of the lease, the lease terminates. Upon such termination, the lessor may recover from the lessee:

(1) The worth at the time of award of the unpaid rent which had been earned at the time of termination;

(2) The worth at the time of award of the amount by which the unpaid rent which would have been earned after termination until the time of award exceeds the amount of such rental loss that the lessee proves could have been reasonably avoided;

(3) Subject to subdivision (c), the worth at the time of award of the amount by which the unpaid rent for the balance of the term after the time of award exceeds the amount of such rental loss that the lessee proves could be reasonably avoided; and

(4) Any other amount necessary to compensate the lessor for all the detriment proximately caused by the lessee's failure to perform his obligations under the lease or which in the ordinary course of things would be likely to result therefrom.

(b) The "worth at the time of award" of the amounts referred to in paragraphs (1) and (2) of subdivision (a) is computed by allowing interest at such lawful rate as may be specified in the lease or, if no such rate is specified in the lease, at the legal rate. The worth at the time of award of the amount referred to in paragraph (3) of subdivision (a) is computed by discounting such amount at the discount rate of the Federal Reserve Bank of San Francisco at the time of award plus 1 percent.

(c) The lessor may recover damages under paragraph (3) of subdivision (a) only if:

(1) The lease provides that the damages he may recover include the worth at the time of award of the amount by which the unpaid rent for the balance of the term after the time of award, or for any shorter period of time specified in the lease, exceeds the amount of such rental loss for the same period that the lessee proves could be reasonably avoided; or

(2) The lessor relet the property prior to the time of award and proves that in reletting the property he acted reasonably and in a good-faith effort to mitigate the damages, but the recovery of damages under this paragraph is subject to any limitations specified in the lease.

(d) Efforts by the lessor to mitigate the damages caused by the lessee's breach of the lease do not waive the lessor's right to recover damages under this section.

(e) Nothing in this section affects the right of the lessor under a lease of real property to indemnification for liability arising prior to the termination of the lease for personal injuries or property damage where the lease provides for such indemnification.

## CC SEC.1951.4 REMEDY PROVIDED BY LEASE; PROVISIONS

(a) The remedy described in this section is available only if the lease provides for this remedy.

(b) Even though a lessee of real property has breached his lease and abandoned the property, the lease continues in effect for so long as the lessor does not terminate the lessee's right to possession, and the lessor may enforce all his rights and remedies under the lease, including the right to recover the rent as it becomes due under the lease, if the lease permits the lessee to do any of the following:

(1)  Sublet the property, assign his interest in the lease, or both.

(2)  Sublet the property, assign his interest in the lease, or both, subject to standards or conditions, and the lessor does not require compliance with any unreasonable standard for, nor any unreasonable condition on, such subletting or assignment.

(3)  Sublet the property, assign his interest in the lease, or both, with the consent of the lessor, and the lease provides that such consent shall not unreasonably be withheld.

(c)  For the purpose of subdivision (b), the following do not constitute a termination of the lessee's right to possession:

(1)  Acts of maintenance or preservation or efforts to relet the property.

(2)  The appointment of a receiver upon initiative of the lessor to protect the lessor's interest under the lease.

## CC  SEC.3308.  LEASE TERMINATED FOR BREACH BY LESSEE; MEASURE OF LESSOR'S DAMAGES

The parties to any lease of real or personal property may agree therein that if such lease shall be terminated by the lessor by reason of any breach thereof by the lessee, the lessor shall thereupon be entitled to recover from the lessee the worth at the time of such termination, of the excess, if any, of the amount of rent and charges equivalent to rent reserved in the lease for the balance of the stated term or any shorter period of time over the then reasonable rental value of the property for the same period.

The rights of the lessor under such agreement shall be cumulative to all other rights or remedies now or hereafter given to the lessor by law or by the terms of the lease; provided, however, that the election of the lessor to exercise the remedy hereinabove permitted shall be binding upon him and exclude recourse thereafter to any other remedy for rental or charges equivalent to rental or damages for breach of the covenant to pay such termination. The parties to such lease may further agree therein that unless the remedy provided by this section is exercised by the lessor within a specified time the right thereto shall be barred.

This section does not apply to a lease of real property unless (a) the lease was executed before July 1, 1971, or (b) the terms of the lease were fixed by a lease, option, or other agreement executed before July 1, 1971.

## CC SEC.3479.  NUISANCE DEFINED

Anything which is injurious to health, or is indecent or offensive to the senses, or an obstruction to the free use of property, so as to interfere with the comfortable enjoyment of life or property, or unlawfully obstructs the free passage or use, in the customary manner, of any navigable lake, or river, bay, stream, canal, or basin, or any public park, square, street, or highway, is a nuisance.

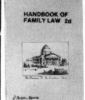
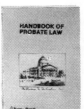

## HANDBOOK OF REAL ESTATE LAW

### IN TWO VOLUMES
By Stuart J. Faber

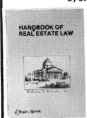

Our newest. Covers sales, escrows, financing, foreclosures, condos, subdivisions, homesteads, brokers, zoning, land use, ownership, liens, syndicates, actions, remedies.

**PLUS FORMS**

**The Price: $31.50
For Both Volumes**

## THE LEGAL STETHOSCOPE

### The Attorney's Medical Handbook
By Samuel J. Faber, M.D. and Stuart J. Faber

A brilliantly detailed and illustrated compendium of anatomy, physiology, injury and disease especially related to the practice of law. An understandable version of those expensive, incomplete medical-legal texts. Plus a legal analysis of medical-legal problems.

**The Price: $19.50**

## REAL ESTATE LIENS ENCUMBRANCES AND SECURED TRANSACTIONS

By Stuart J. Faber

The newest and only book of its kind. Up-to-date text, cases and forms. This book contains the first 11 chapters of HANDBOOK OF REAL ESTATE LAW. If you already have purchased the latter, you don't need this new volume.

**The Price: $13.50**

## HANDBOOK OF GUARDIANSHIPS AND CONSERVATORSHIPS

### Law and Procedure

By Stuart J. Faber

All other books on this subject are out of date. This book treats in detail the 1977 changes on minors and incompetents.

**PLUS FORMS**

**The Price: $16.50**

## HANDBOOK OF LITIGATION FORMS

By Stuart J. Faber

Over 200 forms, including complaints in personal injury cases, real estate, partnerships, many other causes of actions. Motions, demurrers, applications, and many others, some with annotations.

**The Price: $17.50**

## HANDBOOK OF CRIMINAL PROCEDURE 2d

### A Desk and Courtroom Reference
By Stuart J. Faber

This new 250 page California Handbook has been purchased in quantity by DA and PD offices alike. Step-by-step explanations on topics from initial client call from jail to appeals and writs. Includes the latest cases.

**PLUS FORMS**

**The Price: $18.50**

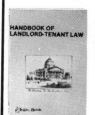
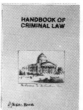

# OTHER GOOD LIFE PRESS PUBLICATIONS

**Good Life Press**
**658 S. Bonnie Brae Street**
**Los Angeles, California 90057**

Dear Sirs:
Please send me _____ copies of book # _____
                     copies of book # _____
                     copies of book # _____
I enclose _____ check or money order.

Name_____

Address_____

_____

Add 70c for postage and handling.